5 ST ROADIE JOB

GET WORKING ON-THE-ROAD WITH TOURING BANDS

Andy Reynolds

© 2019 Andy Reynolds. No part of this book may be reproduced or transmitted in any form or by any means, electronic or mechanical, including photocopying, recording, or by any information storage or retrieval system without written permission from Andy Reynolds, except for the inclusion of brief quotations in a review.

All trademarks are the property of their respective owners.

The author have attempted has throughout this book to distinguish proprietary trademarks from descriptive terms by following the capitalization style used by the manufacturers. Information contained in this book has been obtained by the author from sources believed to be reliable. However, because of the possibility of human or mechanical error by our sources, the author does not guarantee the accuracy, adequacy, or completeness of any information and is not responsible for any errors or omissions or the results obtained from use of such information. Readers should be particularly aware of the fact that the Internet is an ever-changing entity. Some facts may have changed since this book went to press.

ISBN: 9781790862122

Independently published

Contents

Introduction — 6

The Live Music Business Today — 8
The Dominance of Live Music — 9
Opportunities for Getting Road Crew Work — 9
Now is the Time to Start Your Road Crew Career — 10

Step 1: What You Need To Know About The Live Music Business — 12
The Artist and Artist Manager — 12
The Booking Agent — 15
The Concert Promoter — 20
The Show Booking Process — 21
The Contract — 21
The Contract Rider — 26
Tour Budget — 35
Why You Need to know about Tour Support — 38

Step 2: Get To Know The Various Road Crew Jobs — 42
House Crew and Stagehands — 43
Runners — 48
The Artist's Touring Crew — 49
The Suppliers Touring Crew — 52
How to Join these People On-The-Road? — 53
Live Music Business Jobs are Different — 54
Be a Freelancer — 55

Step 3: Set Up Your Own Freelance Crew Business 58

Planning Your Freelance Business	59
Workbook	60
Planning 1 - Where Are You Now?	60
Planning 2 - Where Do You Want To Be?	63
Planning 3 - How Are You Going to Get There?	64
Training & Education	65
Getting Relevant Experience	67
Business Planning 4 - The Legal Bits	70
What Business 'Type' am I? - Your Legal Trading Form	71
Which Business 'Type' to Choose	73
Register a Business Name (AKA "Doing Business As")	73
State, Local or National taxes	74
Business Licenses and Permits	74
Start-up Costs	75
Public Liability Insurance.	76
Cash Flow	77
How Long Will It Take?	79

Step 4: Get Your First Work 82

Get to Know Local Talent	82
Build up Your Network.	84
Use Your Network	86
Getting Hired by People Outside of Your Network	88
Selling Your Services	88
Initial interest. (a.k.a. marketing)	89
Business Buyers Have to Buy	89
Initial Interest from Your Own Web Site	90
Your Own Website	90
Initial Interest Using Email Marketing	101

How to get New Contact Email Addresses	102
Initial Interest Using Social Media	105
LinkedIn	109
Managing your Social Networks.	112
'Brochures'	112
Making a Digital Brochure	115
Résumés	116

Step 5: Do A Good Job and Get More Road Crew Work 122

Clients and Invoicing	123
Rates of Pay	128
Book Keeping	130
Strategies for Getting More Work	132
Get Those Recommendations	136
Testimonials from Satisfied Clients.	137

Conclusion 140

Appendix 1 142

Artist management	143
Booking Agent	145
Concert Promoter	146
Promoter's Rep	148
Tour Manager	150
Production Manager	152
Audio Crew – Systems Tech	154
Audio Crew – Artist	156
Lighting Crew – Systems Tech	157

Lighting Crew – Lighting Director/Operator	159
Video Crew	161
Backline Crew	163
Rigger	165
Caterer	167
Stagehand	169
Driver	171
Tour Security	172
Merchandiser	173
Tour Accountant	175
Wardrobe Assistant	176
Stylist	177
Freelance Crew Contract	**179**
References	**186**
About the Author	**190**

Introduction

So, you want to be a roadie, working with international touring bands? That is fantastic, and myself and my touring colleagues look forward to seeing you out there, on-the-road. Working as a touring technician, tour manager, stylist, or in any other capacity can be a fantastic, rewarding and well-paid life. You will get to share in the excitement of a modern concert - the anticipation, the sense of community, the sharing, and the general appreciation of the good things in life, whist travelling the world and getting paid for it. And make no mistake, live music is big business. The Top 100 Tours of 2018 have so far sold 22.9 million tickets, taking in $2.1 billion [1]. Making those tours happen are the road crew - hard working professionals who share in the glamour and excitement of staging a modern concert. And the road crew are making good money themselves. According to the Wall Street Journal, road crew members are earning up to $200,000 a year, with the most crew people earning about $60,000 [2],which is well above the US household average wage [3].

So how do you join these people on-the-road? How do find out which bands need road crew, and make sure they pick you? How did the existing road crew people get started working for bands on tour? And why are touring road crew jobs rarely advertised? These are all questions you will find the answers to in this book. I am going to tell you how to get fulfilling work by following five simple steps: *Step 1*: Get to Know the Live Music Business, *Step 2*: Get to Know the Various Road Crew Jobs, *Step 3*: Set Up Your Own Freelance Crew Business, *Step 4*: Get Your First Work, and finally, *Step 5*: Do a Good Job and Get More Work.

I have also designed a special workbook to accompany this book, which details the 5 steps, and help you plan out how you are going to get to work on-the-road with international touring bands. You will find instructions on how to access the workbook in Step 3: Set Up Your Own Freelance Crew Business.

And before we begin, I just want to say - Good Luck! There are hundreds of professional road crew, out there right now, working on shows and tours. They are people, just like you, and if they can live their dream of working on-the-road, then so can you!

The Live Music Business Today

The wider music business has been through immense changes in the last decade. In 2007, the Sunday Times declared October 7th of that year 'the day the music industry died', saying 'there is no money in recorded music any more, that's why bands are now giving it away'[4]. If they did give it away, it was only because they could make up their revenue elsewhere - from gigs and touring. The numbers speak for themselves: Live Nation (a concert promoter) has already sold 85 million tickets this year, for a total gross of s $3.8 billion [5]. A Rolling Stone magazine survey of the richest musicians noted 'the vast majority of artists [in our Top Thirty] made the bulk of their cash on the road. Album royalties pale in comparison'. U2 were the richest in 2017, grossing $316 million from touring, despite disappointing sales of their last album. 'In today's world artists have to tour to make money. They can't just sit at home and collect their royalties and expect to make their mortgage payments,' says Gary Bongiovanni editor of Pollstar, a music business magazine [6].

The Dominance of Live Music

On a smaller scale, independent artists such as Snarky Puppy, Zoe Keating, and Tei Shi, make much of their income from performing live. Chance the Rapper, a highly successful independent artist, is now able to tour arenas, with no record company backing (figure 101). He came in at number 94 in the Pollstar Top 100 tours of 2017, selling $445,000 tickets at an average of $48.00 each [7]. It is not just a question of cash. The perceived increase in the importance of concerts and touring for artists has had a massive effect on the nature of the music business in general. Live Nation, the concert promoters who did not even exist 12 years ago, signed U2, Nickelback, Shakira, Jay-Z and Madonna to '360 degree' deals that see the artists and Live Nation share revenue not only from concerts and touring but from the recordings and artist merchandise. In signing these artists Live Nation has directly challenged (and acquired artists from) the established recorded music giants such as EMI, Universal and Sony[8].

There are other examples of the continuing dominance of live music. I have worked with unsigned and independent bands who sell out 1000 capacity venues, spreading the word on the back of solid touring and online activity and all without the backing of a record company or even any physical record sales. Young bands, signed or not, are touring from the beginning of their careers, increasing numbers of venues are hosting live music, and more people are directly employed in the live music industry.

Opportunities for Getting Road Crew Work

So, bands and artists are hitting the road in order to make money. What has that got to do with you trying to get a road crew job? More artists on the road means more opportunities for work. In any major city on any given night there are numerous artists performing live –

Figure 101: Chance The Rapper, an example of a DIY artist.

artists employing sound, lighting, and backline technicians.

Now those bands performing each night may have a full tour crew or just someone helping to do the driving and carrying the road cases. In either case, someone is getting paid to work for an artist. Have a look yourself – go to www.pollstar.com (figure 201) and search your nearest city for tonight's date (simply type a city into the 'search' bar at the top of their web page). There will be a list of at least 5 shows in your town this evening; five bands who will be employing road crew. This basic research should show you that there is a substantial amount of road-crew work out there.

Now is the Time to Start Your Road Crew Career

There has never been a better time for you to start your road crew career. There are more opportunities for work - either in the tried and tested road crew positions (tour manager, sound engineer etc.), or in jobs that have been created in response to technological changes (for instance, radio frequency, or RF, technicians who deal with handling wireless equipment on large tours, have found themselves hotly sought after in recent years). This book is going to give you the background information you need to help you become part of this fast-growing business, with specific advice on getting your first road crew work, and information on how to then turn those first jobs into a career.

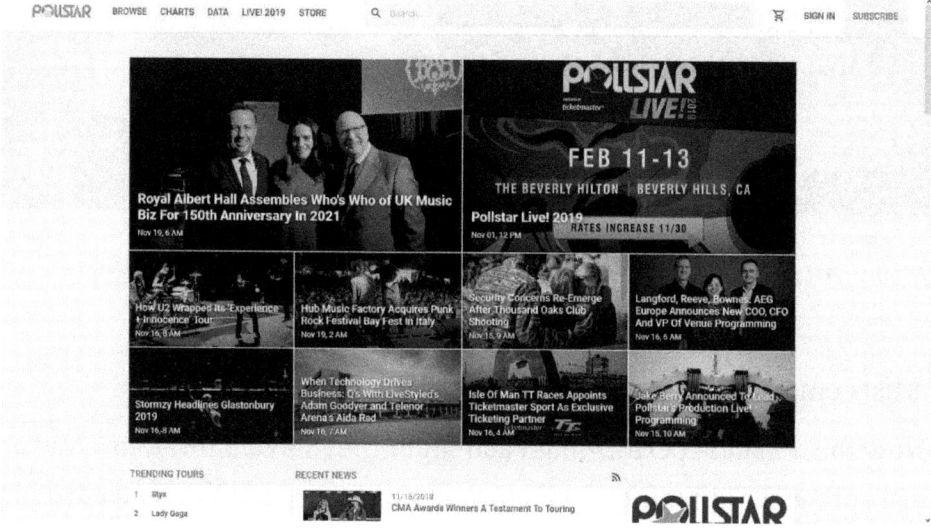

Figure 201. Use Pollstar to do some basic research on how many artists are on tour right now.

Step 1: What You Need To Know About The Live Music Business

You are entering a new area of employment. It's going to help you greatly if and you have a good idea of how this business works, not least because it affects the who and how (and how much) of getting paid for your work! Figure 102 shows the relationship of the key people involved in the live music business - the artist, artist, manager, booking agent, and promoter - and how you will fit into this relationship. Let's start your examination of the live music business by looking at each of these key players in turn.

The Artist and Artist Manager

Everything in the live music business revolves around the artist. 'Artist' in this case means the band, singer, DJ, duo, turntablist - any type of contemporary music artist who is going to perform live. In the early days of an artist's career, it is the artist themselves who gets the gigs - they find venues who are willing to book them in for a show. As an artist becomes more successful - and busier- an artist manager will become involved. Also

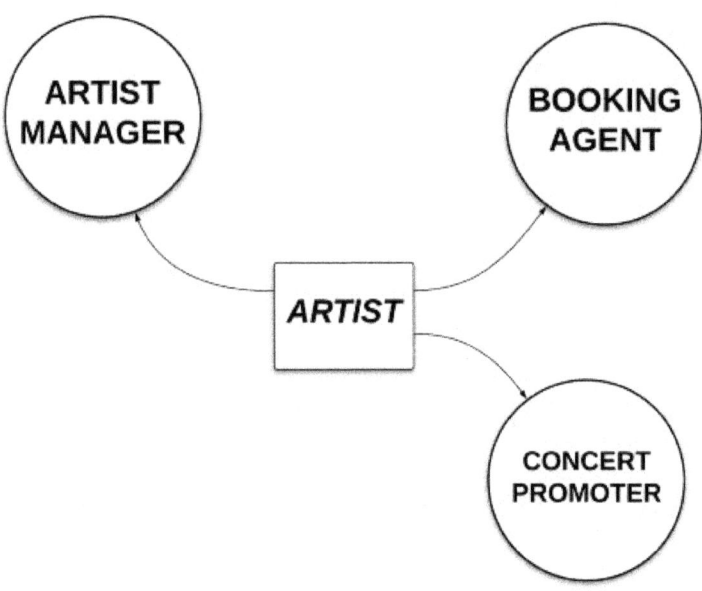

Figure 102: The key players in the live music business

known as the personal manager, she is central to the artist's career. The manager's job is to represent the artist in all business areas and to guide the artist towards the best logistical and financial decisions. This guidance role extends to recordings, publishing, and non-performance promotional activities, but it is the role of the artist manager in shows and touring that is relevant to you here. It is my experience that it is the manager who is responsible for the hiring (and firing) of the road crew, and they are also responsible for setting how much you will be paid.

Managers handle an artist's affairs in return for a percentage (called 'commission') of the artist's gross earnings. The commission rate is usually between 10 and 20 per cent of the artist gross earnings. So, if an artist makes $500,000 from recorded music sales (!), the manager on a 20% commission rate would earn $100,000 from those sales (20% of 500,000 = 100,000). Make note that this example is a for 'gross commission' rate - the manager takes her percentage 'off the top', before other costs are deducted. A gross percentage commission rate is not the best deal for the artist, especially for live performance income. For example, say an artist is touring, and the artist's gross income from all the ticket sales is $40,000 for 10 shows. Let's also suppose that the costs for the tour - wages, transport, accommodation and other live production costs - are $38,000 (touring is expensive). The profit, therefore, is $2000 and this goes to the artist. If the manager then charges 20% of the *gross,* the tour costs are in fact $46,000 - $38,000 + $8000 managers' commission. This is not an ideal position for the artist as they are now losing money - $6000 to be exact. So ideally the manager should charge a *nett* commission rate - only taking their percentage on whatever is left after all expenses have been paid. In this case that would be 20% of $2000 = $400. Not great for the manager, and an incentive for her to reduce costs as much as possible.

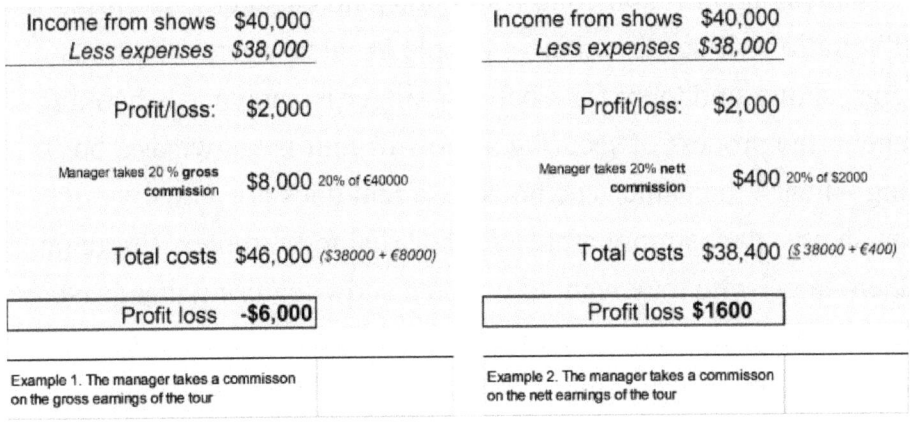

Figure 202. *A diagram showing the effect of gross or nett manager commission on touring income. The managers commission type will indirectly affect your wages!*

This is in fact what happens for most artist managers nowadays

- they charge a nett commission, and so are very keen to reduce touring costs. Unfortunately, the biggest cost on tour is wages - your salary. You must remember this when negotiating your daily rate or salary for a tour.

I mentioned that playing live is expensive. You may stand in a gig, surrounded by hundreds of ticket payers, and think that the artist is making a lot of money. They may be, and they will also have huge costs for each show or tour - wages, transport, accommodation, and other tour production expenses, that quickly eat away the money made from ticket sales. So, as well as finding lots of gigs for the artist, the manager needs to find the money necessary to go out and play live. In the early days, most managers will have to book shows and negotiate performance fees for their artists themselves; after a degree of success (or perhaps signing to a record company), the artist management will likely work with a booking agent.

The Booking Agent

A talent agent is someone who finds paid engagements (film, TV, radio writing) for creative people. A talent agent who finds gigs, shows and tours for a band or singer is known as a booking agent; the process of securing a show or tour is known as a booking – hence the name. The booking agent does not actually put on shows; they simply represent the artist to promoters (more on them later) who may want to put on a show featuring that artist. Booking agents have become very powerful in the last 20 years, due to the increased importance of live performance and the amount of money it generates for an artist. It is true to say that an artist cannot simply hire a booking agent - the agent will contact the artist, as and when the artist is capable of earning sufficient money for the agent.

A booking agent makes money by charging her client (the artist) a percentage of that artist's gross income for the performance. The percentage the booking agent charges is known as the commission, in a similar way to that of artist management commission. This commission rate is universally set at 10 percent for contemporary live music - rock, pop, alternative, what have you, and 15% for DJ work; I shall explain the reason for the higher rate later. This percentage rate may be a convention, and has some precedent in US regulation; the US entertainment unions--AFM (American Federation of Musicians), and SAG-AFTRA (the entity formed after the merger of the American Federation of Television and Radio Artists and the Screen Actors Guild) have set talent agency commission at 10% for all talent agents, including booking agents.

There is no official regulation in the UK concerning agency commission rates, but 10 percent seems to be the norm for 'traditional' artists, and this is probably in recognition of the official rates set by the US unions.

The Pollstar 'Booking Agency Directory 2018 Summer Edition' lists 640 worldwide booking agents [9]. These range from the multi-national, 'full-service' agencies, such as WME and CAA, down to the single person agencies. These very small agencies will usually specialise in a genre, such as blues, or electronic music, and will maybe service a local college or university, finding and booking local and regional acts into that venue. At the other end of the scale are the full-service agencies. The major booking agencies based in the US (but operating worldwide) include:

- Creative Artists Agency
- WME
- Artists Group International
- United Talent Agency

- Paradigm
- Howard Rose Agency

These agencies represent the majority of artists in the Pollstar Top 100 tours - in 2014, 72 of the TOP 100 tours were represented by those six booking agencies alone [10]

Major booking agents in the UK include:

- Coda
- Primary Talent
- ITB
- X-Ray Touring
- MN2S
- Little Big
- Echo Location

The booking agent works closely with the artist manager to plan the touring schedule for the artist and, having agreed a period of touring or concert activity, the agent will approach promoters and offer the artist's services. The agent will attempt to secure a guaranteed fee (the 'guarantee') for the performance as well as a percentage of profits if the show sells a lot of tickets (the 'back end' or 'breaking percentage'). It is the agent's job to negotiate the deals with the promoter based on what she knows of the act's status, the city or venue she is pitching to, and the relationship with the promoter.

When the agent has provisionally booked the act into various cities, she will inform the artist manager of the dates on offer and the fees expected. If the manager approves the tour, the agent will issue contracts to the promoters. The agent will then be available to answer any further questions or concerns the manager or promoters may have before the tour and will act as a go-between should any disagreements arise during the tour itself.

It is very rare to work with a touring contemporary touring artist who does not have a booking agent and I have no doubt that booking agents are the most powerful people in today's live music business. You are well advised to make friends with as many agents as you can in order to gain and keep work in the touring industry.

Figure 302 (overleaf): The various music venue types, with examples, and the type of promoter usually associated with each venue.

TYPE	DESCRIPTION	AUDIENCE CAPACITY	EXAMPLE	IN HOUSE PROMOTION	OUTSIDE PROMOTION	IN HOUSE SOUND AND LIGHTS	MUSIC SHOWS PER WEEK	SHOW TYPES
Bar, pub		20-80	Anywhere!	Yes. Owner or manager, 'hobby' type interest	Very occasionally	Maybe basic PA. Maybe no stage!	2 or 3	Djs, local bands, 'talent nights', tribute bands
Music bar or pub		81-300	The Lexington, London, England or The Bowery Electric, NY, NY	More dedicated promotions team	Occasionally	Basic PA & lights. Stage	5 to 7. More a dedicated business	Local bands, smaller touring acts. Talent night and tribute bands
Music Venue		301-1000	Leadmill, Sheffield, England or Mercury Lounge, NY, NY.	Yes but lots of outside rent	Yes. National promoters	Good PA & LX backstage rooms etc. Options to bring in production	4 to 7	Touring acts, showcases, discos & theme nights at weekends
Theatre/large club		1000-2000	Rock City, Nottingham, England or 9:30 Washington, D.C.	Occasionally unless privately owned	Yes. National promoters	PA for disco events but probably have to rent in all sound and lights	4 to 6	National touring acts, showcases.
Large theatre		2001-5000	O2 Acdemy Brixton, London or Roseland Ballroom, NY, NY.	Occasionally	Yes. National promoters	No existing PA or lights	3 to 4	National touring acts, one offs and multiple runs
Sheds	Ampitheatre with seated and open areas.	5000-15000	Gexa Energy Pavilion, Dallas, TX	Occasionally	Yes.	Very basic	3 to 4 seasonal	National touring acts
Large halls	Part of purpose built venue i.e. university or arena complex	5001-10000	Alexandra Palace, London	Promoter may own venue i.e. Live Nation	Yes.	No existing PA or lights	1 to 3	International touring acts and multiple runs, sporting events
Arenas		10001-30000	The o2, London England or Madison Square Garden Arena, NY, NY.	Mixed. Some festivals run by national promoters	Mixed. Some festivals run by national promoters	No existing PA or lights	1 or 2	International touring acts and multiple runs, sporting events, ice events
Outdoor	Festival and green field sites plus larger 'sheds'	25000-50000 per day	Roskilde, Reading & Leeds, Coachella	No	Yes	No	1 - seasonal	International touring acts
Stadiums		25000-100000	Wembley Stadium, London, Feyenoord, Rotterdam, Mel Life Stadium, East Rutherford, NJ	No unless venue owned/operated by promotion company	Yes	No	1 - seasonal	Superstar touring acts

The Concert Promoter

In the UK and Europe, these people are known as promoters; in the US they are also known as talent buyers. Whatever the terminology may be, these are the brave souls who decide they can make money out of putting on a show or event.

The concert promoter's goal is simple: put bums/asses on seats. This means the promoter takes an artist, puts her into a suitable venue, and sells tickets for the concert to the public. The promoter then makes a profit after paying the artist, and various costs to stage the concert. Some venues manage their promotions (in-house), but usually venues are hired by a promoter to stage a show. Figure 302 shows a breakdown of venues and the type of promoters.

There is an enormous risk involved with concert promotion, and a good promoter will look at turning a profit over the long term by developing good relationships with the artist and their booking agents. A good relationship with the agents means direct access to the agent's roster, her more successful acts. The major concert promoters [11], as reported by Pollstar, include:

- Live Nation – 29,500 concerts in 40 countries in 2018.
- AEG
- OCSEA – based in Mexico City and the largest concert promoter in Latin America
- T4F – based in Brazil
- SJM Concerts - UK
- Frontier Touring - USA
- Chugg Entertainment - Australia
- MCD - Ireland

- FKP-Scorpio – Germany
- DF Concerts - UK
- Goldenvoice - a division of AEG

A quick look in your local or regional gig listings will also show you many concert and festival promoters not listed above, and you will encounter all sorts of in-house, regional and national promoters when you start working for bands on tour.

The Show Booking Process

The artist manager, booking agent and promoter work together to book shows and tours. Promoters will be approached by a booking agent (or manager in the early days of the artist career) to see if the promoter wants to put on a show featuring an artist. The promoter will examine the costs involved in putting on the concert or club night, and the profit potential for him and the artist. The booking agent may well have a figure in mind for the performance (the guarantee), and it us up to the promoter to work out whether he can afford to pay that amount and still make a profit. This profit is dictated by the ticket price, times the amount of tickets that can be sold, less the costs for staging the concert - supplying sound, lights, stage etc. Figures 402 and 502 show you some example show costings.

The Contract

Two documents become important at this stage - the contract and the contract rider. Once the promoter and booking agent agree on the guarantee, the ticket price and the promoter's costs, the booking agent will draw up a show contract, specific to that concert, and send it to the artist and the promoter.

VENUE CAPACITY	150
TICKET PRICE	$10
GROSS POTENTIAL	$1,500
VENUE HIRE (MANAGER, BAR STAFF, CLEANER ETC)	$175
TICKET PRINT	$50
POSTERS, FLYERS, NATIONAL ADS ETC	$50
SECURITY PEOPLE X 2	$160
SOUND ENGINEER	$100
LIGHTING PERSON/ASSISTANT NIGHT MANAGER	$100
OPENING BAND 1	$100
OPENING BAND 2	$50
CATERING	$50
	$835
GUARANTEE TO ARTIST (OFFERED BY PROMOTER)	**$500**
(TOTAL PROMOTER EXPENSES	$1,335)

Figure 402: The costings a promoter will use to decide on how much to pay an artist for a show

They should sign it to agree to the terms. After signing, the contract is returned to the booking agent and the concert is now officially happening. This process is repeated for all the promoters involved if a tour is being put together - contracts are sent out to the individual promoters, who sign to agree to the date, ticket price, venue and guarantee, and then return the contracts to the booking agent. A standard concert contract deal will usually stipulate the promoter agrees to the guarantee, plus will supply 'sound, light, and catering' at their own cost. Figures 602 a & b show a sample show contact.

The show booking process will take place at least two months before the show takes place, so that the promoter has plenty of

VENUE CAPACITY	150
TICKET PRICE	$10
GROSS POTENTIAL	$1,500
VENUE HIRE (MANAGER, BAR STAFF, CLEANER ETC)	$175
TICKET PRINT	$50
POSTERS, FLYERS, NATIONAL ADS ETC	$50
SECURITY PEOPLE X 2	$160
SOUND ENGINEER	$100
LIGHTING PERSON/ASSISTANT NIGHT MANAGER	$100
OPENING BAND 1	$100
OPENING BAND 2	$50
HEADLINER CATERING AS PER RIDER	$100
	$885
GUARANTEE TO ARTIST (ASKED BY BOOKING AGENT)	**$650**
(TOTAL PROMOTER EXPENSES	$1,535)

Figure 502: In this case the promoter will lose money if they pay the artist the guarantee and rider costs being asked for by a booking agent.

time to market the event. Tickets may not go on sale to the public until one month before though. Have a look at concert listings in your area and see how far in advance the concert is taking place to see this for yourself.

Contract No.: **1234**

An Agreement made the 01st day of APRIL 2019
Between P. **Romoter pp TKN Concerts, 123 Gig Street, London** hereinafter referred to as the 'Promoter' of the one part
AND **Ron Decline pp Bum Gravy** hereinafter referred to as the 'Artiste' of the other part.

WITNESSETH that the Promoter hereby engages the Artiste and the Artiste agrees to the engagement to appear/perform as **Bum Gravy** at the venues(s), on the dates and for the periods and at the salary stated hereto.

SCHEDULE

The Artiste agrees to appear at ONE (1) performance as follows:

At the:	**Metal City**
	1 Talabot Street
	Nottingham
	N1
On the:	**Saturday, 11th December 2019**
Capacity:	**1000**
Ticket price:	**£15.00 in advance**
For a salary of: receipts (after £4990.00 costs)	**£5000.00 plus PA/lights + catering vs 80% of door**

SPECIAL STIPULATIONS
1) The exact running times for this engagement are to be advised.

Signed _____ Date _____

This agency is not responsible for any non-fulfilment of contracts by Proprietors, Managers or Artists but every reasonable safeguard is assured.

Figure 602 a & b (and overleaf): A live performance contract. It is specific to that show.

Contract No.: 1234 continued

2) Payment
The guaranteed fee for this engagement is £5000.00 vs 80% of door receipts, after costs, which is payable to the Artiste as follows:

a) A deposit of 50% of the fee, i.e. £2500.00, is payable to by certified check to TKN CONCERTS CLIENTS ACCOUNT and should be posted to TKN Concerts, 123 Gig Street London. **Deposit due immediately on receipt of contract**. In the event of cancellation by the Promoter, this will be retained by the Artiste.

For the purposes of this clause time is of the essence.

b) The balance of the fee, i.e. £2500.00, plus any percentage payments due, is payable to the Artiste in cash pounds Sterling on the night of the performance.

c) The fee should be net and free of all local taxation.

3) Sound and Lights.
Promoter are to provide and pay for a first class P.A. and Monitor system and Lighting systems to the Artistes specification and approval (see attached technical specifications). All the necessary crew is to be in attendance throughout sound check and for the duration of Artistes entire performance.

4) Sponsorship and Endorsement.
The name or logo of Bum Gravy or any of its members shall not be used by any sponsor or be tied to any commercial product or company, nor there be any sign, banner or advertising at or within 30 meters of the stage throughout the entire engagement. Promoter is specifically prohibited from associating Artistes name with any product or sponsorship or promotion whatsoever without Artistes prior approval and written consent.

5) Merchandising.
The Artiste shall have the exclusive right but not obligation to sell souvenirs, posters, programs, shirts and all other merchandise directly pertaining to and/or bearing the likeness of the Artistes at the engagement and to retain ALL monies received from the sale thereof.
Promoter shall ensure that there is sufficient space for suitable stands to be erected for this purpose at no cost to Artiste.

6) Unauthorized recording.
a) The Promoter agrees that no part of the performance may be taped, filmed or otherwise recorded in any way whatsoever. Promoter shall place a sign at the entrance(s) to the engagement which clearly states this limitation.

b) Promoter shall ensure that no recordings take place and shall confiscate or otherwise detain any sound or visual recording materials by visually screening all persons attending the engagement for any recording equipment. Promoter agrees to cooperate fully with Artistes to prevent such recordings and agree to act promptly and diligently to all Artistes requests in fulfilment of this clause.

c) It is agreed and understood that in no instance whatsoever will the Artistes allow filming recording or broadcasts of any type at the aforementioned venue (by persons known or unknown) including but not limited to TV, film, radio, video tape and digital media unless the Artiste gives their prior written consent.

7) Decline to perform
The Artiste reserves the right to decline to perform without prejudice to the full agreed fee in the event of any reason beyond the control of the Artiste including but not limited to strike, lock out, war, fire, serious or dangerous weather conditions.

Signed_____ Date_____

The Contract Rider

The other document that becomes important in the show booking process is the contract rider. You will know the term 'rider' in relation to the food, booze, and red M&Ms that bands are given in their dressing room (as in 'where's the rider?' and 'that support band drank all the rider'). However, the term 'rider' refers to every aspect of the band's touring needs, from truck parking spaces to humidity onstage. Whereas the contract serves as an agreement that is particular to an individual performance, the contract rider is an agreement for every performance to which the act is contracted, regardless of any other consideration. This document 'rides' with the contract, hence the name.

The rider basically says, 'For us, the artist, to do a really good show, we really need the following items, and you, the promoter, have to supply them at your own cost.' Remember the 'sound, light, and catering' agreement in the contract? The contract rider should tell the promoter what sound, lighting and catering the band will require. Figures 702 a to h show a typical contract rider.

BUM GRAVY EUROPE 2019

CAST & CREW

Bum Gravy are **9** people:

<u>4 x band</u>

<u>1 x TM/FOH engineer   Andy Reynolds</u>
Contact: T: +44 (0)7762 551886   E: andy.reynolds@livemusicbusiness.com

<u>1 x Driver   D. River</u>
Contact: T: +44 (0)7777 12345   E: sprinter@merc.com

<u>1 x back line technician   C. Himp</u>
Contact: T: +44 (0)7777 98765   E: chimp@hotmail.com

<u>1 x lighting engineer   Ms. L. Ampy</u>
Contact: T: +44 (0)7777 90909   pulsarrules@aol.com

<u>1 x merchandise seller   S. Wag</u>
Contact: T: +44 (0)7777 00700   isithereyet@yahoo.co.uk

Millions of Americans are NOT travelling with a monitor engineer. The purchaser agrees to supply one sound engineer(s) who is capable and willing of mixing monitor sound for Millions of Americans, at no cost to the artist.

Cast and crew will travel together in one (1) vehicle as listed below. This vehicle also contains all the backline and lighting equipment.

PREPARED BY ANDY REYNOLDS - TOUR MANAGER
T: **+44 (0) 7762 551886**
Email: andy.reynolds@livemusicbusiness.com

THIS RIDER EXPIRES AUGUST 30th 2019

Figure 702a: The first page of a contract rider - a general document for every show an artist performs.

1. ACCESS AND EQUIPMENT

The Purchaser agrees to provide and pay for 2 (TWO) able bodied and sober persons to assist the Artiste with the get in and get out of the Artistes equipment. The Purchaser also agrees to provide 1 (ONE) runner with own reliable transport.

The Purchaser agrees to allow access to the venue/ performance space at a reasonable time as specified and agreed by the Artistes Tour Manager. Artiste reserves the right to supplement certain sound and lighting equipment after consultation with the Purchaser; in such cases the Purchaser will provide and pay for a fully qualified electrician and provide and pay for all necessary sound and lighting operatives necessary to assist in installation of supplementary sound and lighting equipment.

2. PA and LIGHTS

See separate technical rider for Artistes specific requirements.

Millions of Americans are carrying their own In Ear Monitor system (IEM). This operates on 832.700 MHz (EBU CH 66) and be altered between 830 to 866 MHz. For full details please see attached technical specifications and/or contact Andy Reynolds on +44 (0)551886 or email andy.reynolds@livemusicbusiness.com
Millions of Americans are carrying their own lighting system which will complement the existing venue lighting system. For full details please see attached technical specifications and/or contact Ms. L. Ampy on +44 (0)7777 90909 or email pulsarrules@aol.com

3. PARKING

The purchaser agrees to ensure parking space for:
1x Mercedes Sprinter band splitter van VRN # STA 456
This parking space should be adjacent to venue load in and be secure and free of cost to the Artiste.

PREPARED BY ANDY REYNOLDS - TOUR MANAGER
T: +44 (0) 7762 551886
Email: andy.reynolds@livemusicbusiness.com

THIS RIDER EXPIRES AUGUST 30th 2019

Figure 702b

4. MERCHANDISING

The Purchaser agrees to allow the Artiste sole right to erect stands for the sale of merchandise, in a clean and well-lit area, at no charge whatsoever to the Artiste.

5. GUEST LIST

The Artiste reserves the right to admit up to 10 guests free of charge and this will not prejudice the Artistes fee. Purchaser agrees to confirm numbers of Purchasers own guests with Artiste's Tour Manager before opening the venue to the public.

6. SETTLEMENT

The Purchaser agrees to provide all documentation relating to the Artiste's performance for the inspection by Artiste and Artiste's Tour Manager. This documentation including but not limited to pre - sale ticket reports, show cost receipts, on night ticket sale reports and tax exemption submissions should be available at time of settlement, usually one hour before completion of Artiste's performance. The Purchaser agrees that all relevant show costs should have corresponding receipts and that failure to provide original receipts will result in corresponding cost to be null and void.

7. SECURITY

Purchaser agrees to provide and pay for adequate numbers of reliable and reputable security personnel with clearly marked apparel and identification. Such personnel should report to designated security manager who in turn follows instruction from Artiste's Tour Manager. Purchaser agrees to co-ordinate with security manager and Artiste Tour Manager regarding particular security arrangements, pit crew etiquette and instruction.

The Purchaser shall always guarantee proper security to ensure the safety of the Artiste, auxiliary personal, instruments and all equipment, costumes, vehicles and personal property during and after the performance. Security must be provided in the areas of the stage, dressing room and all exits and entrances to the auditorium, mixing consoles and Artiste merchandising stalls.

PREPARED BY ANDY REYNOLDS - TOUR MANAGER
T: +44 (0) 7762 551886
Email: andy.reynolds@livemusicbusiness.com

THIS RIDER EXPIRES AUGUST 30th 2019

Figure 702c

Security protection is to commence upon arrival of the Artiste on the premises, until equipment is re-packed into transportation and Artiste personnel have left the premises.

Artiste will provide laminated passes that shall be sole accreditation valid on day of Artiste's performance. Artiste's Tour Manager will approve and issue sticky passes for all non- - touring personnel. The Artiste reserves the right to refuse any accreditation issued by Purchaser or venue.

8. SUPPORT/ OPENING ACTS

The Artiste reserves the right to approve and or amend support/-opening acts. The Purchaser agrees not to add other acts other than those approved by the Artiste in writing.

The Artiste reserves the right to dictate the running order of the show and the acts appearing therein. The Artiste reserves the right to advise or amend any music, film or performance relating to the Artiste's performance including but not limited to intro music, play on music, after show DJ's and video compilations.

9. CATERING AND HOSPITALITY

The Purchaser agrees to provide the following:

Clean and hygienic toilet and sanitary facilities, including 2 (two) showers with hot and cold water available all day, must be provided. If these are not available within the venue/ performance area, arrangements must be made at a local hotel (or other) facility.

Dressing Room (band)
This room must be clean, well lit, furnished and lockable and in a secure area. 220v outputs and sufficient furniture (including full-length) for a minimum of eight (8) people. Adequate climate control or heating control in winter months is essential.

PREPARED BY ANDY REYNOLDS - TOUR MANAGER
T: +44 (0) 7762 551886
Email: andy.reynolds@livemusicbusiness.com

THIS RIDER EXPIRES AUGUST 30th 2019

Figure 702d

Security protection is to commence upon arrival of the Artiste on the premises, until equipment is re-packed into transportation and Artiste personnel have left the premises.

Artiste will provide laminated passes that shall be sole accreditation valid on day of Artiste's performance. Artiste's Tour Manager will approve and issue sticky passes for all non- - touring personnel. The Artiste reserves the right to refuse any accreditation issued by Purchaser or venue.

8. SUPPORT/ OPENING ACTS

The Artiste reserves the right to approve and or amend support/-opening acts. The Purchaser agrees not to add other acts other than those approved by the Artiste in writing.

The Artiste reserves the right to dictate the running order of the show and the acts appearing therein. The Artiste reserves the right to advise or amend any music, film or performance relating to the Artiste's performance including but not limited to intro music, play on music, after show DJ's and video compilations.

9. CATERING AND HOSPITALITY

The Purchaser agrees to provide the following:

Clean and hygienic toilet and sanitary facilities, including 2 (two) showers with hot and cold water available all day, must be provided. If these are not available within the venue/ performance area, arrangements must be made at a local hotel (or other) facility.

Dressing Room (band)
This room must be clean, well lit, furnished and lockable and in a secure area. 220v outputs and sufficient furniture (including full-length) for a minimum of eight (8) people. Adequate climate control or heating control in winter months is essential.

PREPARED BY ANDY REYNOLDS - TOUR MANAGER
T: +44 (0) 7762 551886
Email: andy.reynolds@livemusicbusiness.com

THIS RIDER EXPIRES AUGUST 30th 2019

Figure 702e

2 x large trash/rubbish bins.

Twenty (18) large, clean towels with soap required from sound check time

Oil lamps, incense, candles, drapes and flowers are all welcome and should be included to improve the ambience of the environment.

Support band Dressing Room (TBC)
As above (see separate rider for catering/towels etc)

Production office
A secure production office that can be locked with telephone, desk, chair, Ethernet/CAT 5 cabling, and/ or Wi-Fi connection. (Please supply access codes, network keys etc), RJ111 phone sockets and 220v power will be required wherever possible.

Please provide the production Tel/fax numbers ASAP in advance

Crew Room
As band (no mirror required) – 10 (10) towels and soap at load in.

PREPARED BY ANDY REYNOLDS - TOUR MANAGER
T: +44 (0) 7762 551886
Email: andy.reynolds@livemusicbusiness.com

THIS RIDER EXPIRES AUGUST 30th 2019

Figure 702f

Catering

At load in time (13.00) for 5 people (crew plus driver(s)):
Constant hot tea & coffee set up (with biscuits etc)
Bottled still mineral water (Volvic, Spa or Evian)
Assorted Coca - Cola (no Pepsi!) Dr. Pepper etc
Assorted fruit juices (cranberry, orange, apple etc)

From 16.00 (4PM) band dressing room (drinks on ice):
8 x fresh vegetarian sandwiches (or sandwich ingredients plus bread)
24 x good quality local/imported bottled beer
20x l litre still mineral water (Volvic, Spa or Evian)
Assorted soft drinks, fresh OJ, apple juice, cranberry juice, Cokes etc
1 bottle of good quality local wine
1 x litre bottle quality vodka (Stoli, Findlandia, Moskosavoya etc NO ABSOLUT!)
Constant tea, coffee and hot water set up
Lemons and honey
Tissues, chocolates and chewing gum assortment

At 18.00 (6PM) main meal time for minimum nine (9) people (including 2 vegetarians) A covered dining table in a clean, smoke free and warm location (not the dressing room) with metal cutlery, appropriate crockery and condiments. Some band members may elect to eat after the show and this facility must be available. Drinks should be re-iced as required.

NOTE:
A hot, nutritious meal is always preferable. Should there be no alternative a buy-out of £10/€ 20 per person is acceptable. Please check with the Tour Manager in advance.

PREPARED BY ANDY REYNOLDS - TOUR MANAGER
T: +44 (0) 7762 551886
Email: andy.reynolds@livemusicbusiness.com

THIS RIDER EXPIRES AUGUST 30th 2019

Figure 702g

Food:

Individual place settings with assorted local breadbasket

Choice of starter (hot & cold) plus large fresh washed mixed salad bowl with dressings.

Hot choice of three entrees with vegetables, not limited to:

Vegetarian option (can include pasta)

White meat/ fish option

Red meat option

Sweet dessert course

Please leave some empty boxes in the dressing room to pack items at the end of the night

After show bus supplies:

Hot local take out speciality or pizza (1x vegetarian 1x other)

9 x sodas

PREPARED BY ANDY REYNOLDS - TOUR MANAGER
T: +44 (0) 7762 551886
Email: andy.reynolds@livemusicbusiness.com

THIS RIDER EXPIRES AUGUST 30th 2019

Figure 702h.

I mention riders as they have an impact upon the amount of money the artist will make for a show. This in turn will affect how much the artist can pay you. To explain, we need to go back to the show booking process for a moment. When planning to stage a concert the promoter will work through the finances, much as shown in figures 402 and 502, and propose a financial offer to the artist (in the case of a scenario such as figure 402), or agree to the guarantee asked by the booking agent. Promoters profits are small, compared with the artist's fees, and concert promoters must work hard to reduce costs. Unfortunately, a big part of any promoter's costs will come from supplying items and services set out in the artist's contract rider - sound, lights, catering etc. You can see what I mean if you reduce the amount set aside for catering, as in in figure 802 - the show will now break even, with perhaps a small profit for the promoter. So ideally the rider should be sent to the promoter, via the booking agent, before the promoter agrees to putting on the concert - so they can include the items listed in their costs. However, due to ever-changing tour personnel and requirements, outdated or incomplete riders are often sent out by booking agents. Any subsequently updated (or late) riders may then contain items that significantly affect the promoter's ability to stage the show under the agreed-upon terms (and within his budget). It is important that booking agents have the latest, sensible rider information from the artist manager before the contracts are issued.

Tour Budget

The booking agent will work with the promoter to finalise the promoters offer. If putting a tour together, she will send all the various promoter's offers to the artist and the artist manager who, once presented with a list of potential concert dates, will have to make sure the tour or show is financially viable for the artist.

Figure 902 shows the type of sheet the booking agent will send the artist for their consideration. Its then up to the artist, with the help of her manager, to work out if she can afford to undertake the tour or not.

VENUE CAPACITY	150
TICKET PRICE	$10
GROSS POTENTIAL	$1,500
VENUE HIRE (MANAGER, BAR STAFF, CLEANER ETC)	$175
TICKET PRINT	$50
POSTERS, FLYERS, NATIONAL ADS ETC	$50
SECURITY PEOPLE X 2	$160
SOUND ENGINEER	$100
LIGHTING PERSON/ASSISTANT NIGHT MANAGER	$100
OPENING BAND 1	$100
OPENING BAND 2	$50
HEADLINER CATERING AS PER RIDER	$50
	$835
GUARANTEE TO ARTIST (ASKED BY BOOKING AGENT)	**$650**
(TOTAL PROMOTER EXPENSES	$1,485)

Figure 802: The promoter has reduced the amount set aside for catering in the artists rider and the show will now just about break even.

I've said it before - playing live is expensive. It may be the case that the guarantees being negotiated by the booking agent are not enough to cover all the expenses the artist will incur from going out on tour. This is especially true for one-off shows and festival appearances. Simply getting everyone together in the same place at the same time can cost a great deal of money: if the guarantee is low it

BUM GRAVY
SUMMER 2019

DATE	CITY	COUNTRY	STATUS	ANNOUNCE?	VENUE / FESTIVAL	PROVIDING	BUYER	FEE
06 August 2019	Copenhagen	Denmark	Confirmed	Yes	Vega small hall (cap 450)	S, L, C	Live Nation	$2,500.00
07 August 2019	Gothenburg	Sweden	Held	Not yet	Way Out West - Sticky Fingers (cap. 400) or Pustervik (cap. 300)	S, L, C	Live Nation	$3,000.00
08 August 2019	Off							
09 August 2019	Berlin	Germany	Confirmed	Yes	Lido (cap 400)	in-house S&L, C	FKP Scorpio	$2,000.00
10 August 2019	Hamburg	Germany	Confirmed	Yes	Knust (cap 500)	in-house S&L, C	FKP Scorpio	$2,000.00
11 August 2019	Cologne	Germany	Confirmed	Yes	Luxor (cap 500)	in-house S&L, C	FKP Scorpio	$2,000.00
12 August 2019	Munich	Germany	Confirmed	Yes	Atomic Café (cap 350)	in-house S&L, C	FKP Scorpio	$2,000.00
13 August 2019	Off							
14 August 2019	Hasselt	Belgium	Confirmed	Yes	Pukkelpop Festival	S, L, C	Live Nation	$2,000.00
15 August 2019	Salzburg	Austria	Confirmed	Yes	Frequency Festival	S, L, C	Nuemusic	$10,500.00
16 August 2019	Erfurt	Germany	Confirmed	18 April	Highfield Festival	S, L, C	FKP Scorpio	$4,000.00
17 August 2019	Off							
18 August 2019	Edinburgh	Scotland	Held	Not yet	Cabaret Voltaire (cap 250)	in-house S&L, C	DF Concerts	$789.00
19 August 2019	Glasgow	Scotland	Held	Not yet	King Tuts (cap 300)	S, L, C	DF Concerts	$1,677.00
20 August 2019	Manchester	England	Held	Not yet	Roadhouse (cap 260)	in-house S&L, C	SJM Concerts	$1,317.00
21 August 2019	Dublin	Ireland	Confirmed	Yes	Marlay Park w/THE KILLERS	S, L, C	MCD	$5,000.00
22 August 2019	Off							
23 August 2019	Reading	England	Held	Not yet	Reading Festival	S, L, C	Festival Republic	$2,961.00
24 August 2019	Leeds	England	Held	Not yet	Leeds Festival	S, L, C	Festival Republic	$2,961.00
25 August 2019	Birmingham	England	Held	Not yet	Academy 2 (cap 350)	in-house S&L, C	SJM Concerts	$1,316.00
26 August 2019	London	England	Held	Not yet	Hoxton Bar and Kitchen (cap 250)	in-house S&L, C	SJM Concerts	$1,316.00
27 August 2019	Off							
28 August 2019	Basel	Switzerland	Confirmed	Not yet	Z7 (cap 1,000)	S, L, C	Sofa Booking	$6,160.00
29 August 2019	Paris	France	Confirmed	Yes	Rock en Seine	S, L, C	Nous Productions	$4,500.00
30 August 2019	Amsterdam	Netherlands	Confirmed	Not yet	Paradiso - upstairs (cap 250)	in-house S&L, C	Mojo	$1,925.00
31 August 2019	Ludinghausen	Germany	Confirmed	21 April	Area 4 Festival	S, L, C	FKP Scorpio	$4,000.00
							TOTAL TOUR INCOME:	$63,922.00

Figure 902: The booking agent will send the artist a sheet that details all the promoters offers. The total income figure is the one that is most important to the artist.

may not be worth it. In any case the manager will have to work out the list of expenses the artist will incur from playing the show or tour. This list is called 'the budget', which is a bit misleading as it is more a list of predicted expenses, but you get the idea. Expenses that are included in a budget are:

- Wages - you!
- Transport
- Accommodation
- 'Production' - PA, lights, video, backline, set, staging, work permits and visas etc.

This is not only for stadium headliners - four dudes playing a show in the next city will still need to figure out their expenses - gas for the van, a hotel perhaps, spare guitar strings and paying for the rehearsal room (figure 1002). Whether stadium or bar, the income from the show or tour, minus the expenses the artist may have, will mean either a profit or loss for the artist.

Why You Need to know about Tour Support

You should know about tour support, and how it is paid, if you want to work for bands on tour - the payment of tour support has a direct impact on your salary. To explain: once a budget has been worked out to the manager's approval, a couple of things may happen. If the budget shows a profit, or if the band is not beholden to any record label (in other words, if they are as big as U2, Dead-Mau5, or Ed Sheeran), then the manager will approve the tour and tell the agent to go ahead and confirm the shows.

If the budget shows a loss (called 'shortfall'), then the band can

	Price per day/unit	Days/multiplier	Multiplier		Notes
WAGES					
Tour Manager/FOH engineer	$150.00	14	1	$2,100.00	Tour Manager gets paid for each day of the tour
Backline crew person	$100.00	12	1	$1,200.00	Backline person only gets paid for show days
PER DIEMS					
Crew day off	$10.00	2	1	$20.00	Backline person gets $10 a day on days off
ACCOMMODATION					
Band & crew	$50.00	13	3	$1,950.00	3 twin rooms at $50 a night
TRANSPORT					
15 Seat Passenger van	$150.00	15	1	$2,250.00	Total includes pick up and drop off days
Fuel		15000	miles	$1,205.67	
Trailer	$25.00	15	1	$375.00	
Parking	$5.00	14	1	$70.00	Just in case!
BACKLINE					
Equipment consumables	$200.00	1	1	$200.00	Spare strings and replacement, batteries, sticks etc
			TOTAL EXPENSES	**$9,370.67**	

Figure 1002: The budget for a small headline tour.

either decide not to do the proposed show or tour or try to find extra money from somewhere else. The most common route is to go to the record label (if the artist is indeed signed to a record label) and ask for *tour support.* Tour support is money given to the act by the label to cover the shortfall and enable the act to go on tour. The amount of tour support is negotiated at the time of the recording contract negotiations and is 'recoupable' (it has to be paid back) from whatever money the band earns from their music.

An artist will usually need to apply to their record company for tour support, every time they want to go on tour. This involves submitting a budget to the business affairs department of the record company. If that application is approved, the record company will usually stagger the payment of the tour support, where a percentage of the tour support is paid before the start of the tour, and the remaining amount is payable on receipt of the tour accounts at the end of the tour. And that is where the payment of our support will impact upon you. This final payment can take some time to be approved as all receipts and invoices must be tallied up and submitted to the record companies accounting division. If the record company agrees with how much has been spent, they will ask the artist to invoice them for the reaming percentage of the tour support amount. Your wages, and any expenses you are owed, will probably be paid out of this second chunk of tour support and the artist may not be able to pay you if there is a problem or dispute with those final tour accounts. You will see more about getting paid in '*Step 5: Do a Good Job and Get More Road Crew Work*'.

Step 2: Get To Know The Various Road Crew Jobs

So far, we have met the artist manager, the booking agent, the promoter and the promoter's reps - the people involved in organising a modern music performance. Once that is done, it is the road crew who go out and set up the shows. Figure 103 is my diagram of the various road crew jobs, and how they apply to a venue that has its own promoter or a larger venue that is dry-hired by an outside promoter. There are three separate groups of crew involved in putting on a concert - the house/stagehand crew, the artists touring crew and the suppliers touring crew. The following pages will help you explore the roles of each, especially the artist touring crew - as this is the kind of work you really want!

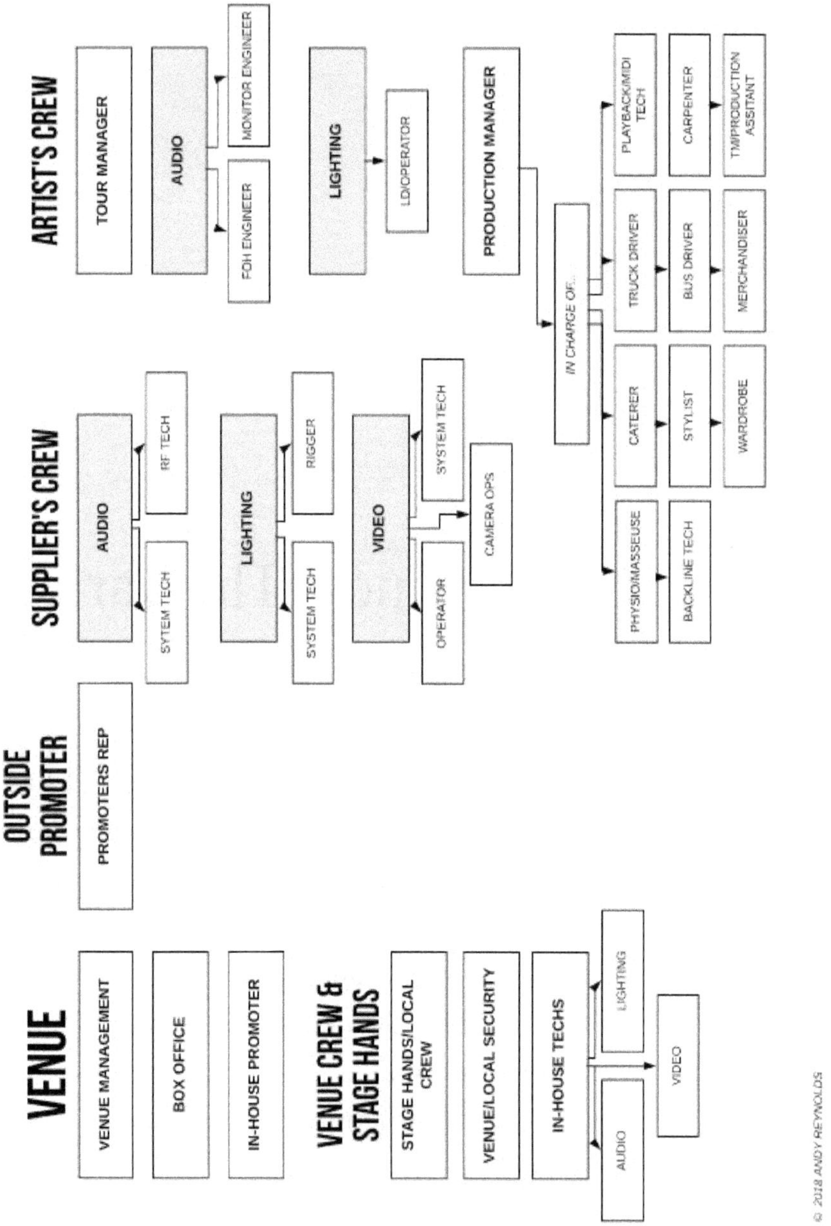

Figure 103: The various road crew jobs.

House Crew and Stagehands

The first of the three type of road crew is the house crew/stage hands (known as 'local crew' in the UK)

House crew work for the house - that is the venue. Look at the table of venue types in figure 302 again. You can see that bars, clubs and smaller venues have their own technical production staff - the house crew. At the very least this will be a house sound engineer who is employed to set up, run, and maintain the venue's sound system in readiness for the visiting artist. House sound engineers often must work with sub-standard or old equipment, and deal with sometimes 3 or 4 different artists a night, 4 or five nights a week. Working as a house technician will teach you to be tolerant and adaptable, as well as short cuts and techniques that will be useful to you on tour. The wages paid to house techs is not very high though, and the hours are obviously quite anti-social (evenings and weekends), without the glamour of international travel. However, many touring road crew got there break by meeting the right artist at the right time while working as an in-house technician. I toured with Dave 'Supa' Rupsch (Katy Perry, Megadeth, All American Rejects, fun, and Panic! At The Disco) after he got his break in 2001, while working at the venue of Missouri State College, and he has toured extensively since [13].

So, small to medium venues will have their own in-house techs. All venues will also use stagehands, another crewing option you should explore. Stagehands are employed, usually on a temporary, hourly basis, by the venue or the promoter, specifically to assist the touring or visiting crew with the loading in and load out of the PA, lights and the musicians own equipment (The musicians equipment is known as the 'back line' and consists of the speaker cabinets, amplifiers, drums, cymbals, keyboards, guitars, pedal boards and stands that the band use on stage). On large theatre, arena, and stadium shows, stagehands will also be employed to load in all the set, staging, lights, PA, wardrobe, catering, and production equipment, as well as the back line. A typical arena-type show will involve about 20 to 40 stagehands for each load in and load out. Working as a stagehand is a great way to learn how a modern concert 'works', and to meet your future touring network.

The work of a stagehand is hard, involving long, unsociable hours of physical labour. You will be unpacking and packing trucks, shifting huge flight cases about and running heavy cables around venues. Physical strength is useful, but stamina is the more important trait. Stagehands are not paid very well, as the work is considered low-grade manual labour, but the job offers two important benefits for someone looking to get into freelance road crew work - an insider's view of the various methods and equipment used in modern touring, and direct contact with touring personnel.

Stagehands are charged out to the visiting production on a time basis called a 'call'. A call is usually four hours. This means each stagehand must be paid for four hours of their time, even if their work is finished sooner. On a typical concert you might work for four hours in the morning (load in) and then not work again until the call in the evening (load out). However, the more capable stagehands will often be retained after the morning call. They will then assist with setting the stage, loading in and assisting opening acts. These stagehands are known as 'stop-ons' (so called because these stage hands 'stop on' when the other crew have already been released). Being a stop-on means even longer days but more money, and more intimate contact with the artist's touring crew. Touring crew will soon notice the individual stagehands that possess relevant technical skills or training, that work hard, are sensible, and have a good attitude. They will get those stagehands moving away from the straight forward unpacking and packing of trucks. These stagehands will instead be assigned more interesting tasks throughout the set-up process of the show, working alongside the touring crew. The most common role for these 'stop-ons' will be to assist the back line techs load in and set up the back line. This gives the stagehands one-to-one, direct contact with the bands own crew. Make a good impression here and you will have made a very good connection into future touring work! (When I load into a venue, I always ask the stagehand crew boss to assign the more capable and intelligent of his crew to me directly. I can then work with those stagehands, directing them to assist my sound and lighting department heads, knowing the stagehands have the relevant knowledge to really help my crew.)

All major concert cities will have at least one crewing agency or union 'local' who will supply stagehands to promoter's and venues. Make the necessary enquiries and sign yourself up for this kind of work. Most crew agencies insist that you are self-employed and are responsible for paying your own taxes. Many venues in the US are regulated through IATSE (International Alliance of Theatrical Stage Employees, Moving Picture Technicians, Artists and Allied Crafts of the United States), and non-members are therefore not allowed to load/unload their own equipment (figure 203). The unloading, loading, and carrying of all the visiting production equipment must be done by a workforce designated by the local union. You will have to join a 'local' union in order to be able to crew at venues covered by IATSE in your city (a directory of local unions can be found at http://www.iatse.net/member-resources/local-union-directory)

Once on the books of the organisation you should make sure you get employed on as many shows as possible. This may be difficult for you as many major cities have venues spread far and wide –

Figure 203: IATESE. You might need to join to work as a stage hand in your city (US only)

you may find yourself working on shows 20 miles from where you live and travelling for an hour or more to and from work at unsociable hours. I have found that the responsible agency or union will try to allocate the more local people to particular venues; it makes sense to the agency as they want you to be able to be home early enough to get up and work on a show the next day.

Once you find yourself working regularly on local events you should buy yourself an 'AJ' (adjustable spanner - see figure 303) and plenty of PVC tape (figure 403). The AJ will be used to bolt the lighting truss together. Modern concert lighting is hung from a sub-structure, or 'grid', which is suspended from the roof of the venue/stage. This sub-structure is made up of sections of 'truss" – lightweight sections of metal frame. These sections need to be assembled before the lights can be attached and the grid hoisted into the air. This is the first job of the day for any touring production and therefore will be one of the first jobs you will do after unpacking the truck - hence the AJ. The PVC will be used to wrap up the cables

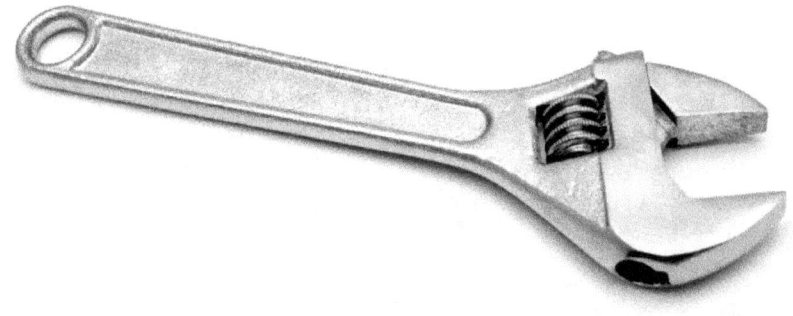

Figure 303: An AJ, or adjustable spanner, used to bolt lighting trusses together. You should buy one for your first stagehand jobs.

properly at the end of the night. Having these two basic tools on you, for every show you do, shows you understand the job you have signed up for, and that you are not there just to throw boxes into a back of a truck for a (part-time) living. Finally, you should observe closely what is going on when on a call and ask lots of relevant questions.

Runners

Another type of stagehand is the runner. The equivalents of 'gofers' (as in 'go for this, go for that') from the film world, runners are local people with access to transportation who can go on errands for the band's production personnel.

The runner will make herself known to the arriving production during load in and will put up a blank shopping list in the

Figure 403: PVC tape - used to tie up the cables used in modern concert touring.

production office or dressing room, along with her cell number. If the touring crew needs something during the day, such as musical equipment spares, photocopying, batteries, or laundry, they either phone the runner or write their requests on the list in the production office, along with along with their name. The runner will then go and purchase whatever is necessary, having been given a cash float by the tour manager or tour accountant.

Working as a stagehand or runner is a great introduction to the long hours and hard work involved in concert production but is not a touring job. You need to be part of the artist's own crew in order to go on tour.

The Artist's Touring Crew

The second group of people you need to know about is the artist's touring crew. These are the jobs you really want - working directly for the artist.

Music artists will rely on the house crew to take care of the sound engineering and lighting when they first start out playing shows, in their home town for instance. As they begin to play more shows, the artists may then look to have some continuity in the sound and lighting for their shows. They will get this continuity by employing sound engineers, lighting operators and others, to then travel with them for every show they perform. These people form the artist's own touring crew and may initially consist of a sound engineer and tour manager. More people will be employed as the artist becomes more successful, performing in larger venues for bigger guarantees. More money means they can employ more people! Working for the artist directly means you have a better chance of touring, perhaps internationally, and you will earn more than either house crew or stagehands. The following is a brief description of the most common artist crew jobs and you can find more information about these, and other touring roles, in the appendix.

Tour Manager

The tour manager is hired by the artist to take care of all the advance planning of the tour - booking transport, accommodation, finding crew etc. She then travels with the band on the tour itself, taking care of the day-to-day running of each show. The tour manager's job on-the-road varies enormously depending on the type and success level of the act for which she is working and is hard but rewarding work. Tour managers are often responsible for the hiring or recommendation of new road crew as well, so it pays to make a good impression, especially if you find yourself working with an opening act - get a business card to the headliners tour manager if you can!

Audio Crew

At the very least a band will employ a Front of House (FOH) engineer to travel with them. In the early days of their career, the artist's FOH engineer will work alongside the house sound engineer at each show. As the artist grows in popularity, they will play bigger venues and they, or the promoter, will hire in a PA ('public address' - another word for the sound system) if no existing sound system is in place - in sheds, large halls, and arenas for instance. In that case there will be additional audio crew who work for the PA supplier and arrive with the sound system. You will examine the role of this supplier crew later, and what it means in practice is that there will be two separate groups of sound crew working on the show - the artist's own FOH and monitor engineer, and audio crew supplied by the PA rental company.

Lighting Crew

Touring with a lighting director (LD) is a significant investment for an artist - she must be touring in venues that have lighting equipment worth having a specialist come in and operate, or festival slots after dark, or both. Touring with lighting equipment raises the game even further - taking lighting into small and mid-capacity rooms (500-2000 person) adds a whole load of logistical considerations (lighting can take a long time to be rigged and programmed) and will add to the tour costs. Having bitten the bullet however, a good LD can elevate a mundane show to a dazzling (literally) new level.

As with audio, the LD will work alongside the in-house lighting person in the 'early' days of the artists touring career. It may then become necessary at some point to tour with lighting equipment - either to supplement the existing house rig to provide the artist's distinct visual identity, or because the venues on the tour have no lighting systems in place. This is 'production' touring (taking production into venues) and the lighting crew will be split into two sets in the same way as the audio crew--usually one LD who works directly for the artist, and house/system crew who work in the venue or tour with the rented lighting rig.

Backline Crew

These are the boys and girls who tend to the personal instruments, amplifiers, electronics and effects of the musicians themselves. Back line crew, or technicians, are also known by their allotted responsibility on stage, so you have 'bass techs', 'drums techs', 'keyboard techs' etc.

Back line techs are the jobs with most band contact and are the types of jobs that most people associate with being a roadie. While it is true that back line tech for a successful band is almost like being in the band itself, with first class travel, nice hotels and a personal relationship with band members, there is a great deal of responsibility in making sure the equipment works every night, regardless of the conditions. Jonny Bass Player may be your best friend on tour, and wait until he has a bad gig, his equipment stops working and you can't fix it, and then see if you really are 'friends'...

The Suppliers Touring Crew

Our third set of road crew people is the suppliers touring crew. If you examine the venue chart again you notice that larger venues do not have existing PA or lights installed - this equipment will have to be bought in for each show or event. It therefore makes sense for the band to take the same PA and lighting on tour with them if they are playing a series of these types of venues; using the same system every night means a consistent look and sound to the show. Artists very rarely won their own PA, lighting and video systems - they will rent them for the duration of their tour. As I mentioned before, taking PA and lights along is known as 'production touring', as there is a complete production - PA, lights, video, as well as the bands back line, on the road. Accompanying the touring systems will be the supplier crew (or 'system techs'), who work for the supplier and are there to assist the bands crew in rigging, operating and de-rigging each system.

Suppliers usually specialise in one area of expertise so, for instance, there will be a PA supplier who will send along three system techs with their PA, the lighting supplier, also sending along three system techs with their system, the video supplier etc. The system techs are freelancers (I will explain freelancing in the next section), who are hired by the supplier on a tour-by-tour basis. It is good, proper touring work, and not to be dismissed. However, being a system tech means longer days than the artist crew, and a lot of responsibility, not only for the equipment, but in making sure the bands own crew are happy as well.

I have worked as all three - stagehand, system tech and artist crew - and being a member of the artists own crew on tour is the best position!

How to Join these People On-The-Road?

You should now have a complete picture of who does what on-the-road and, more importantly, how the concert industry works. This understanding is important – knowing your industry will stand you in a better position when you come to finding work. However, you still do not know how these people get started or how *you* can get a touring job. And, I bet you have probably done some searching around for these jobs to try and find out. You might have spent any time searching the help wanted ads, in newspapers or on line, and found that ads for road crew positions are rarely placed. Yet, in any major city on any given night there are numerous acts playing – acts employing all the sound, lighting, back line and management crew you have examined previously. You used Pollstar.com to see that there is a substantial amount of road-crew work out there. But why are these jobs not advertised?

There are three reasons. Firstly, the artists and their management companies do not wish to be bombarded with resumes and enquiries from the general public and wannabees. The music industry is a small network serving a vast number of artists; this industry simply does not have the time and resources to sift through the hundreds of (probably irrelevant) applications a traditional job ad would generate.

Secondly, the skills, experience and personality required for a road position are specific to the hiring band or tour. The total number of people qualified for any given position on a tour is probably 20 – 30, worldwide. It is not cost effective to advertise a job to such a tiny number of suitable applicants.

The third, and main, reason is that the positions the artist needs filling are not really jobs as you understand them.

Live Music Business Jobs are Different

In order that you understand why live music business jobs are different, you must understand that the economics of a touring artist do not allow for the hiring of full-time staff. The majority of artists do not make enough money from touring to retain permanent employees, despite the increase in revenue from live work. They hire their tour crew as and when they are out on tour. The 'jobs' in the live music production business are therefore short-term, non-permanent positions, offered on a contract basis. And, as you have learnt, these contracts are not advertised, as it is just not cost-effective.

To put it another way, a live sound engineer may be touring with an artist for two solid years, and once that artist goes off the road (to record a new album or for a break), the artist won't want to be paying that live sound engineer a monthly wage for work the engineer is not doing. The engineer must find work with another artist, on another tour. No tour crew person can make a living working only for one particular artist as there simply is not enough permanent work. Therefore, the only way to work effectively and earn a decent living in the live music business is to be a freelancer.

Be a Freelancer

The Oxford English Dictionary describes freelance as 'earning money by selling your work or services to several different organisations rather than being employed by one organisation.' A recent study indicates that 40% of Americans will be freelancers by 2020, so you are not going to be alone!

In any case, freelancers are self-employed. That means you are your own boss. Most tour crew, including me, work as self-employed freelancers, and we are free to choose when we work and for whom. However, as we are self-employed, we have to search continuously for employment. And you will too. Today's multibillion-dollar concert industry requires that, to get the work, you must know more, be better trained and be more professional in your approach than the next guy. This approach therefore goes beyond replying to help-wanted ads and sending out résumés in order to get a 'job". Your route into road-crew work needs to be appropriate to the nature of the industry.

You need to set up your own road crew freelancing business.

Step 3: Set Up Your Own Freelance Crew Business

You need to treat your career as a business, so you can get work on the road with touring artists and, more importantly, keep working on the road with touring artists. You don't need to rent an office, hire a receptionist and start a multi-national corporation. You *do* need to become self-employed though, and being self-employed means you do not have an employer to look out for you – you are responsible for making your own money, keeping your own books and accounts, issuing contracts of employment, taking out insurance and paying your own health care bills and, most importantly, paying your own taxes. These are not responsibilities to be undertaken lightly. Failure to organise your finances, taxation and insurance obligations properly can lead to business failure, bankruptcy and even a prison sentence. However, treating your freelance career as a business will enable you to be organised, legal and successful. You need to plan your business to do this - the following section will help you do so.

Planning Your Freelance Business

There are numerous helpful books and websites dedicated to starting your own business. A quick search for books on online will return results about specific books on self-employment and freelancing in the creative industries. In the USA you should also go to the Small Business Administration website (www.sba.gov); in the UK the SmallBusiness site has similarly useful information (www.smallbusiness.co.uk). One thing that all business start-up guides will agree on is the need for you to make a business plan.

There is an accepted form for business plans, which usually includes, amongst other things, the key management, organisational and financial data for the proposed business. And, while I agree with the need for a plan, I would say to you that you do not need to produce a 10,000-word document complete with marketing plans and a 5-year profit forecast! You are starting a freelance tour crew business, not launching a multi-national conglomerate - so keep your business plan relevant and realistic for the live music business. Your business plan should be a road map - your route to success and a reminder of where you are going if things start to go wrong. Your plan should therefore be simple, starting out by looking at where you are in your life, your relevant skills and experience, planning where you want to be in the future and how you are going to get there.

Figure 104: The Small Business Administration website (USA only).

Workbook

I have created a workbook to help you plan out your freelance road crew business. You should download it here: **www.livemusicbusiness.com/workbook** . You could print it out, and it's quite long, or you can have it open on your computer of tablet and fill in the details. It is important that you spend some time filling out the workbook - you need to set down your vision for where you want to be in the future. By writing it down, you will have a record of your goals and ambitions, and you can refer to this record if things get a bit rough and you become discouraged. The workbook is set out in sections - *Where Are You Now, Where Do You Want To Be, How Are you Going To Get There*, and *Planning the Legal 'Bits' of Your Business.*

Planning 1 - Where Are You Now?

There is no better place to start a plan than having a good look at where you are now. These questions are fundamental to starting your planning process and have asked them of yourself previously, using the answers to perhaps convince yourself that you could not possibly work on tours with international touring bands. And, if you thought that, you were wrong!

Age

It does not matter how old you are. Certain activities, such as driving a rental van, or hiring equipment, may mean you have to be a certain age, and in my experience, there is no lower or upper limit to road crew work - as long as you are fit and healthy and willing to do what it takes to get the show on-the-road. Certainly, experience usually comes with age, and so your past experiences may put you in a good place to help younger artists. You will find it tough to get road crew work if you are over 40 with no previous experience and that does not mean it will be impossible. Working as a stage hand will make you plenty of direct industry contacts and you should pursue this line of work as an older person.

Location

Location may have a bearing on your new road crew business. Although you are going on tour, and so could really live anywhere, it will be useful to you in the early stages of your new career to live near to somewhere that has a recognised music scene. Cities and towns with a vibrant music scene will often have concert production companies and people living there also - these people are then in a good place to service the music events taking place. The limitations of living in a remote place does not mean you have to immediately move to Nashville, New York, or London, and you should spend some time carefully researching the existing concert production companies, venues and crewing companies in or near your home town. You may have to consider relocating after doing this research, especially as a great deal of your early work will be with local bands and venues, which will be difficult if your home town has little of either.

Again, the results you get from searching on Pollstar.com will give you some idea of the amount of concerts and events that are happening near you, and therefore how much demand there is likely to be for road crew.

Driving License

Touring requires driving - a license to do so is therefore invaluable! Even though most of the band touring takes place on a sleeper bus, with a supplied driver, you will still find yourself having to drive equipment vans, splitter vans, rental cars and maybe even small trucks in your road crew duties. If you don't have a driving license then make sure you build in the time, and the cost, for getting one, in your road crew business planning.

Passport

Have you got a passport? Now this may seem a far-fetched question, especially if you have never travelled outside of your own state, let alone to a different country. But a modern music tour will take its band and crew to foreign countries, and those countries will need to see your passport in order to let you in. You therefore need to get your passport if you are serious about going on tour as a crew person and build in the time and the money to do so when planning your road crew business. Obtaining a passport should be relatively easy, just time-consuming and costly. The cost of a new US passport is currently $145 [14]. And remember, you have to apply for a passport, it is not a right.

The obvious reaction for you as new crew person is to say, 'I will wait until I actually need a passport, then I will apply for one'. This is a mistake; a tour manager will want to know you have a passport before offering you work on a tour that requires international travel. The tour manager cannot take the risk of your passport application being delayed (or even worse, denied) before the tour starts and so will want to know that you have a valid passport when offering work to you. (Touring in some countries also requires applying for work permits and visas, all of which require each member of the touring party to have a valid passport. Applying for work permits and visas must take place before the tour starts - often 2 or 3 months in advance. You must have a valid passport at the time these visas are being organised in order to be considered for the tour). Plan your passport application process now.

Planning 2 - Where Do You Want To Be?

This is your chance to dream, and really explore, about where you see yourself in 1 year, 3 years or 5 years You should spend some time filling out this section of your workbook - you need to it will be good for you to set down your vision. You can also refer to this record if things get a bit rough and you become discouraged. So, what are you aiming for? What's your dream job or role in the concert touring business? Write it down!

Are you interested in sound, or lights? Are you perhaps more interested in becoming a backline tech - fixing and setting up guitars, or perhaps maybe drum kits, or show programming using Ableton Live? Or you may want to be a concert tour manager? Whatever your dream, you should write it down in this section of your workbook. You will then have it written, in big bold letters!

Planning 3 - How Are You Going to Get There?

You have identified where you want to be, and now you need to set out your plan of how to get there. This next section of your workbook will involve examining your current skill 'set' and identifying areas you need help or training in.

Skills

The skills relevant to the concert touring industry are primarily those that deal with setting up and maintaining the equipment used by touring bands - the back line, sound and lights, set and staging. It therefore makes sense for you to have some of those skills, and if you haven't got them, know where to get them. You might have relevant skills already. For instance:

- Can you play an instrument?
- Can you string a guitar, set up an amp with a 'power soak', or set up a drum kit?
- Can you record a live band using Pro Tools, arrange a session in Ableton Live, or cable up a MIDI controller?
- Do you own, or can you drive a van or truck?

These are examples of some of the basic skills that will help you to get work. You might also have sound engineering or lighting operation skills, both of which will also help you get road crew work. In any case, you should identify your current 'skill set' - what you know and are able to apply to modern concert touring - and then identify areas of knowledge you lack, or that you feel you could improve.

Use step 3, lesson 5 in the workbook to research and record your current skill set ('current relevant skills') and skills you feel you may need ('further desirable skills'). Concentrate on a maximum of five relevant skills for now, and perhaps another five desirable skills you would like for the future.

Training & Education

By filling in the worksheet for lesson 5 of step 3, you should hopefully have identified areas where you may want to improve skills you already have or learn new, relevant ones. Your next task is to identify what training or education you need in order to make those improvements. Training and education are important to your career progression, and care should be taken in choosing the right course or qualification (not least because good training is expensive!). As a by-product, the fact that you have studied and gained a qualification also shows that you have commitment and dedication - you so should always mention relevant training when approaching employers or clients. But what training or education do you need?

Colleges and courses do exist to teach technical stage craft for theatre environments (figure 204); a quick search in Google will turn up courses and colleges in your area. (Search for show production courses, stage management courses and theatre technical training). I have also found degree courses in event management which will teach you some of the skills necessary to become an effective band tour manager. It is important to also have an understanding of the management behind the industry you work in, so make sure you have fully understood the lessons in *Step 1: 'What You Need To Know About The Live Music Business'*.

As you are entering the live music business, which involves people *listening* to live music, the most useful courses to look at might be something to do with live audio engineering. There are many audio engineering courses that are studio/producer based i.e.

the making and mixing of MP3s and CDs. The audio theory may be the same for recording and mixing for CD's or radio and live audio engineering and there are huge differences in the conventions and protocols of live audio production. To get the most out of any audio course, you should look for those that specialise in audio for live music events or show production.

I teach live sound and I say that any course in live audio you undertake should cover the following areas in some detail:

- Power – understanding voltage and amperes, different power cables and connectors, and the implications of working with 3-phase power.
- Sound – how sound travels, the frequency spectrum and frequency wavelengths, Inverse Square Law as applied to audio.
- Signal path – Ohms Law, gain structure, microphone and line level amplification, inserts and auxiliaries on analog consoles, desk bussing and grouping on analog consoles, output, multi-core, stage boxes, remote boxes.
- Signal cables and connectors – XLR, NL2, NL4, NL8, EP5/6, handling and storing cables.
- Networking for live audio - audio transmission networks including Dante.
- Microphones – dynamic and condenser microphones, microphone pick-up patterns, phase reversal.

Use the worksheet in step 3 on training and education to make notes about 5 courses or colleges that you can find. Write down the details in the workbook, along with notes on the cost, entry requirements and other factors that will determine your choice of training or education.

Figure 204: There are many colleges and universities that offer course and training in live audio.

Getting Relevant Experience

A problem with starting out in a job or training is that you do not have the experience that makes you invaluable to your clients. It's the same old scenario - you can't get the work until you have the experience and you cannot get the experience until you have worked in the industry...

Luckily however, you can work on shows and events doing jobs that do not require much (if any) experience. These roles are ideal as a starting point to further your freelance career and I thoroughly suggest you try to experience at least one of them, in order to see how a modern concert works, from the inside. The two roles I suggest that will get you t experience are stagehand and merchandise seller.

Stagehand

You have examined the work of a stagehand in step 2 and you know that all major concert cities will have at least one crewing agency or union 'local' who will supply stagehands/'local crew' to promoter's and venues. You should therefore make the necessary enquiries and sign yourself up for this kind of work.

Crewing companies advertise in trade directories and on line, and so should be easy to find and contact (figure 304). Unions are slightly different, but you can have a look at the IATSE website (refer to Step 2 for information on IATSE), or simply ask around during the load-in or load out at a major venue that uses unionised labour to find out the best way to go about joining. Get employed on as many shows as possible once on the books of a crewing organisation. This is obviously easier said than done - working as a stagehand is low-paid, physical work, completed usually during unsocial hours. You perhaps need to commit yourself to a period where you will work as a stagehand - over the summer on music festivals for instance. Stagehand work great way to experience modern concert touring and increase your network. So, make your application and set aside a couple of months to do as much of this kind of work as possible. Many of my university students take as much crew work as they can after exams and during semester breaks, to get plenty of experience. The extra money doesn't hurt them, either!

Merchandise Seller

The other, very useful, service you can offer straight away is that of selling the band's merchandise, or 'merch'. The merchandising operation for most bands is their financial lifeblood and every artist I have ever worked for has told me how important it is to them to have someone capable and trustworthy to look after their merchandising operation. And, for you, the selling of the merch means you get to work on shows, maybe even getting paid for your work. Then you will perhaps go on a tour – with little or no previous

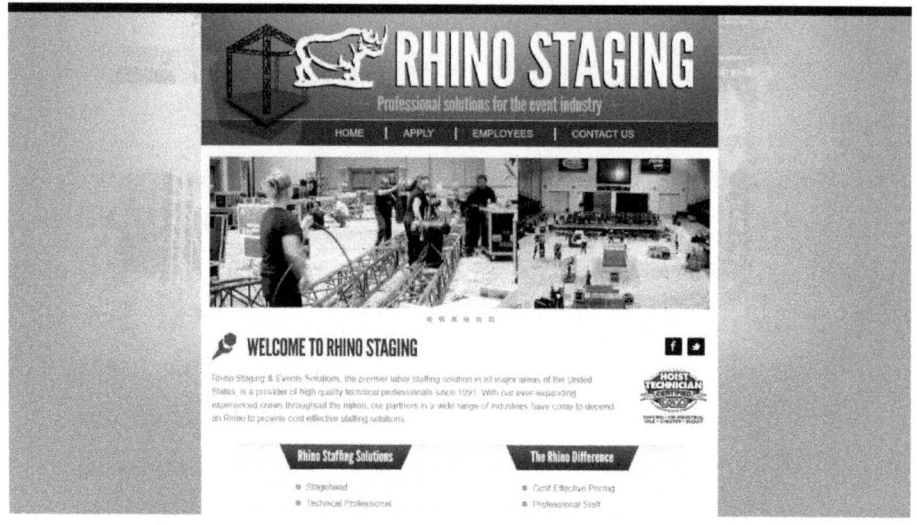

Figure 304: A stagehand crew agency

experience of touring. Don't sit back and coast along when this happens though - you need to capitalise on the opportunity. Offer to help wherever you can, and not just with the merch selling. You are only busy as a merch seller after the audience is let into the venue, so during load-in, sound check, and load-out you are free to help out - helping the artist you are with, the other acts on the bill, the tour manager, the promoter – whoever.

If you can't find an artist to directly sell merch for then you should approach the companies who print and supply t-shirts, posters etc. For touring artists, companies such as Bravado (figure 404) and Manhead, always need freelance merchandisers to take care of sales on-the-road for the artist they represent. Working for the merch company means you would not work directly for the artist and you therefore may not get to meet or make friends with them, but merch selling still leaves you lots of time in the day when you can make yourself useful to the tour manager and crew.

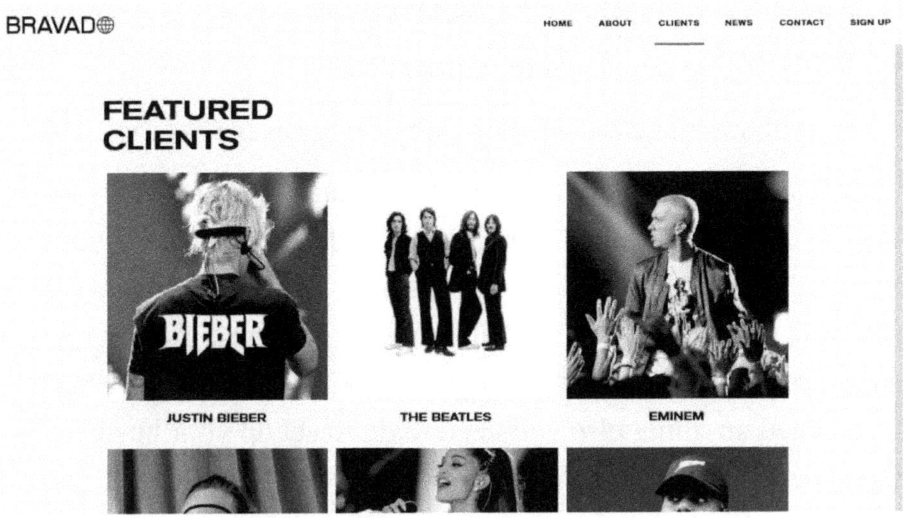

Figure 404: Bravado is a full-service merchandising company that prints and distributes merch for touring artists.

Business Planning 4 - The Legal Bits

You have so far identified where you are, where you want to be and done some research on how you are going to get there. You ultimately want to set up your own road crew business, working with bands on tour. Setting up the business requires this planning and requires that you comply with certain legal stuff. Don't worry though, none of it is too hard, or expensive, to do - if it was then there would be no small businesses!

What You Need To Do

All business books and sites tell you that you will have to do some, or all, of the following to start your business, depending where you live:

- Choose a business location
- Determine the legal structure of your business

- Register a business name ('doing business as')
- Register for state, local or national taxes
- And obtain business licenses and permits as necessary.

I stated earlier that there are numerous online guides you can read to find out specifically what you need to do for where you live. You should go to the Small Business Administration (www.sba.gov) if you live in the US and to SmallBusiness (www.smallbusiness.co.uk) if you live in the UK. Make sure you have researched anything else you need to do to set up your business, again depending on where you live.

Business Location

You do not need premises (an office or workshop) to start your road crew business. In fact, I would totally advise against spending any money on any type of premises for a road crew business. Its money you don't need to spend, especially when you can work from home - as you are going to be touring you need somewhere you can receive mail, make phone calls from, and has an internet connection. In fact, depending on where you live, you may be able to claim use of your home as 'home office', and therefore save money on your tax bill. You should check with your local tax authority to see how this is done.

What Business 'Type' am I? - Your Legal Trading Form

Choose a legal trading structure for your new freelance business. This structure is recognised by the relevant taxation authority and is dependent on the size and scope of your plans for the business. The accepted forms are sole trader, partnership, LLP, and corporations/limited companies/PLCs

Sole Trader/Sole Proprietor

A sole trader/sole proprietor is one person running their own business. Being a sole trader/sole proprietor and is the simplest way to start a business. You keep all the profits from the work you do and are also personally liable for any business debts. This means, that in the event you can't pay bills associated with your business, your creditors (people you owe money to) can seize your personal possessions (your car, your home studio equipment, even your house) in order to get some money from you.

Partnerships

Like two or more sole traders running a company together. Profit is divided between the partners; each partner is also equally liable for any business debt (see 'Sole trader/sole proprietor' above). If your partner runs up business debts and cannot pay, you are as liable as she is.

Limited Liability Partnerships (LLP)

A partnership structure that protects the partners from any liability for the business's debt. LLC's are complex and have costly set-up fees. However, your personal assets (car, home studio, house) cannot be seized to pay for company debts. Many music business partnerships - lawyers, artist managers, sound designers etc. - form LLPs to give them some small protection from the uncertain living they may make in the music business.

Corporations/Limited Companies/PLC's

Very simply these companies are owned by the shareholders – the 'boss' works for those shareholders, does not directly receive the profits and cannot sell the company. However, management and employees are not liable for the company's debts. Limited companies/PLCs and corporations are expensive to set up and have onerous legal and taxation responsibilities.

Which Business 'Type' to Choose

I would advise starting your freelance business as either a sole trader/proprietor or partnership. All you need is to choose a trading name, inform your taxation authority that you are now a sole trader (very important) and you are in business! As your business grows you can change the type and that should not be necessary until you perhaps must employ other people in your business.

Register a Business Name (AKA "Doing Business As")

Giving your business a name, other than your own, is tempting and highly unnecessary. You do not need to adopt a corporate identity - you will be a sole trader and therefore should trade as that. Besides, even adding 'Sound Engineer' or 'Crew Services to your real name as part of your business identity will mean you will have to comply with certain legal obligations in order to let people know that you are 'doing business as' another name. For instance, if your name is Anna Golden, and you call your company, 'Anna Golden Tour Management,' you are 'doing business' as that name, and not as Anna Golden - you may have to then register that name ('Anna Golden Tour Management') which is time consuming and may cost money, depending on where you live. I would therefore avoid a fictitious name and simply trade as yourself, i.e. Anna Golden. This avoids confusion and may also make domain name registration for your web site easier - more of this in a later step.

State, Local or National taxes

Working for yourself, and running your own company, means that you are responsible for making sure you pay your taxes - there is no employer to take the tax out of your pay packet for you. Registering for income, state and local taxes should be straight forward - again, if it was not then no businesses would do it!

Once registered you should make sure that you put enough aside out of each payment you receive you for work done in order to pay your tax when it is due. For instance, here in the UK the basic level of tax is 20%. When I receive payment for a tour or show, I put 20% of that money in a separate bank account and do not touch it until my tax bill is due at the end of January each year. I can then pay any tax I owe, without worrying about it or being late with my payment. Failure to pay tax is usually an offence and can lead to fines, or prison. Please read all the necessary information about income and business tax that is relevant to where you live.

The good thing about running your own business as a sole trader or partnership and being responsible for paying tax is that you 'pay yourself first' - that is, no tax is taken from the payments you receive. If you are careful, put some money aside and keep good records, you may be able to reduce the amount of tax you are due to pay - more money for you than if you worked for someone else!

Business Licenses and Permits

As well as a 'doing business as' permit, you may also need other license and permits to carry on your road crew business. Check with your local authority, state license office or chamber of commerce to find out what, if anything, you may need. Touring road crew work does not need any kind of other business license or permit in my experience, but you never know - so do the research and find out!

Start-up Costs

The good news is that starting your own live music crew business should not cost you a great deal. Certainly, you do not need to manufacture products, hold stock or buy raw materials. There are no employees to hire (yet) and most services you need can be hired by the hour or a similar period. You should write down all your possible start-up expenses and study them to see how you can afford them, however inexpensive they may appear. This will tell you how much money you need to save or borrow to make the jump into self-employment. Figure 504 shows a list of start-up costs. I have used a six-month timescale, as this is a realistic timeframe to get your business up and running.

You may tot up your start-up costs and realise you need more money than you thought. If your savings won't cover the costs you might need to borrow the money. Borrowing should be a last resort and, if necessary, you should look at an overdraft from your bank. Overdrafts are perfect for small business start-up as a they are usually cheap to set up and run, they are usually for small amounts, (a couple of thousand dollars at the most) and are ideal for short-term borrowing. The downsides is that a bank can ask for repayment of the overdraft, in full, at any time. You may also have to guarantee the overdraft - which may mean proving you have steady income - something that is difficult if you are starting a business. As I keep saying, overdrafts cannot be that hard to get, otherwise millions of small businesses would not have them! Just be careful and set a sensible overdraft limit with your bank and you should not run into too many problems later.

CATEGORY	ITEM	AMOUNT	NOTE
Premises			
	Rent	$1,800	Working from home x 3 months
Utilities			
	Gas	$150	x 3 months
	Electricty	$150	x 3 months
	ISP	$90	x 3 months
	Cell	$300	x 3 months
Financial and legal			
	Book keeper	$150	x 3 months
	Public Liabilty Insurance	$400	
Marketing			
	Web site	$90	Domain name, hosting
	Directory listing	$150	x 3 months
	Business card	$75	
Equipment			
		$250	Headphones, Mag-Lite, multi tool etc
Misc			
		$200	Office stuff
	TOTAL	$3,805	

Figure 504: A list of start-up costs for you new road crew business.

Public Liability Insurance.

One cost you must include in your start-up costs is that for insurance, especially 'Public Liability' or 'General Liability' (PL/GL) insurance. Setting up a freelance road crew business means you are liable for medical and legal costs if a member of the public, your client or someone else who works for your client is hurt or killed as a result of something you do while working. Likewise, you are liable if you damage or lose a piece of the client's equipment or property. PL/GL insurance protects you from having to pay these costs if there is an accident. More and more live production suppliers (sound, light and staging companies) now require freelancers they hire to have this kind of insurance. PL/GL insurance can be very expensive, especially for people involved in entertainment industries, and there are several dedicated insurers and trade unions who can negotiate discounts on your behalf. You should Google 'freelance public/ general liability insurance' for a list of companies that deal with PL/GL

Cash Flow

Successful business people always say, 'cash is king' and they are right! A business with plenty of cash can survive even if it is not making a great deal of profit. Conversely a business with no cash reserves will not survive - even if it is making a profit. Your freelance tour crew business will be no different. As an example, figure 604 shows the 'profit' on paper for a business selling $1000 of goods or services a month and with expenses of $500 a month. Looks healthy doesn't it? But the figures do not take into account when money actually comes in to your account and so may be slightly deceptive.

ITEM	Month 1	Month 2	Month 3	Month 4	Month 5	Month 6
Sales	$1,000	$1,000	$1,000	$1,000	$1,000	$1,000
Costs	$500	$500	$500	$500	$500	$500
Sub-total	$500	$500	$500	$500	$500	$500
plus b/f from last month	$0	$500	$1,000	$1,500	$2,000	$2,500
Profit	$500	$1,000	$1,500	$2,000	$2,500	$3,000

Figure 604: A profit statement – looks healthy doesn't it?

Figure 704 shows the same business, measured by its cash flow. This shows when money comes in and goes out of the account. As you can see, the business does not receive any money until month 4, which is common if your client pays you on term of 90-days. This business is going to be in trouble for the first 5 months as there is not enough cash to cover the monthly expenses. 'Cash flow' is therefore the way of measuring when you are going to receive money from the people who owe it to you and when you

ITEM	Month 1	Month 2	Month 3	Month 4	Month 5	Month 6
Sales	$0	$0	$0	$1,000	$1,000	$1,000
Costs	$500	$500	$500	$500	$500	$500
Sub-total	-$500	-$500	-$500	$500	$500	$500
plus b/f from last month	$0	-$500	-$1,000	-$1,500	-$1,000	-$500
CASH	-$500	-$1,000	-$1,500	-$1,000	-$500	$0

Figure 704: The same business, measured according to when money is actually paid into the bank. Costs are the same, but the business would be bust in six months.

need to pay other people for goods and services. It is the lifeblood of your business; plenty of cash coming in regularly means you don't have to worry about paying your bills. Having to wait 30, 60 or even 90 days for your customers to pay you means either a) you must wait 30, 60 or 90 days to pay your bills or b) borrow money to pay your bills. Borrow too much money and you are in danger of still being in debt when you eventually do get paid by your customers.

Pay attention to your cash flow and plan for it before you start your new freelance business, especially if you are going to have to apply for an overdraft. The bank will want to see your projected income, and the cash flow that goes with that. The way invoices are paid is particularly different in the live music industry. My advice would be to assume your invoice will not be paid for at least 90 days, and you have enough cash (or the overdraft facility) to survive that long. A good tactic to keep your cash flow, er, flowing, is to charge a percentage of your invoice up front or (in the case of a long tour) charge weekly. Most artist's business can set you up on a payroll, meaning you get paid each week you are on tour. This is great for your cash flow and you should check to see if your client can do the same.

How Long Will It Take (To Set Up Your Road Crew Business)?

Starting your new tour crew business is going to take time. Don't rush. You are probably impatient to get going but I would recommend you spend at least the next two months researching and planning, and another four months setting up your marketing and your network. Then, in about 6 months' time, you will be ready to start your business properly.

The important thing you should do during the planning and research stage is to stay in work or study - be totally on top of any existing work or school commitments. You don't want to get fired or fails assignments because you were too busy, or ended up too tired, to concentrate on what you already have in place - especially if it's a job that pays your bills. So, stay in school, or at work. You might want to try to find a job with more flexible hours if you see yourself getting a lot of crew work straight away and, in any case, its always worth talking to your boss or professor about what you are trying to achieve. They will be sympathetic, especially if you present a good plan, with a realistic time frame and a well-researched cash-flow forecast. Moving to flexible hours will help you to go ahead and get some stage hand experience, which should be a big part of your plan to go full-time as a touring road crew person. Having flexible hours, or lots of negotiated time off (un-paid holiday for instance) will also enable you to undertake smaller tours for new clients, should you get offered them. You should only 'quit your day job' when you have enough work lined up, and your cash flow forecasts show that you can stay in the black when your last pay check runs out. Figure 804 shows a sensible business planning time line.

This time line is part of your business plan and should never be really finished – it is a road map to help you get where you want to go. At some point you should be confident that your business can work; part of this confidence will come from knowing there are customers out there – customers who are willing to hire you for their tours or events.

<u>6 Months to go.</u>

Research clients. Buy music industry directories. Build Wordpress site and Facebook, Twitter and LinkedIn pages. Hit up network. Register business with tax authority. Make sure on top of existing work commitments. Research any funding. Take on a couple of freelance jobs.

<u>5 Months to go.</u>

Take on more freelance jobs. Find a book keeper and/or accountant. Open business bank account.

<u>4 Months to go.</u>

Continue to build up customers. Do some local advertising and keep the network informed about work. Make sure invoices go out.

<u>3 Months to go.</u>

Get book keeper to chase up outstanding invoices. Check progress of business bank account.

<u>2 Months to go.</u>

Scale back existing job commitments (go part time?). Hit up existing clients for referrals and testimonials. Leaflets and brochure? SAVE ALL CASH!

<u>1 Month to go.</u>

Quit day job! Make sure new clients pay up-front for next two months.

Figure 804: A 6-month time line for starting your road crew business.

Step 4: Get Your First Work

There is no recognised career path, such as an exam you have to pass, for freelance live production crew. However, I know a couple of steps that most crew take to get started. Assuming you have identified your skills, perhaps undertaken some training and got a bit of experience as stage hand or merch seller, you are now in a position to get solid, paying road crew work. To do that, you must get to know local talent. Quite simply: find yourself a local artist and grow with them.

Get to Know Local Talent

There are numerous examples of some guy who knows a small, local band. The band start doing lots of gigs. The guy tags along to all their shows, until the band get sick of him getting in the way and drinking all their beer, so they give him something to do, such as carrying their gear and tuning their guitars (figure 105).

The band get bigger and better shows, go on tour and take their friend with them. Over time, and almost by accident, he becomes a full-fledged road crew person and, when his friends take a break to record a new album, he finds work with another band, touring with them. And It really is that simple. It may not be *easy,* but it is a <u>simple</u> process. You have spent a bit more time and effort on planning your road career than our friend in the story, but the process is the same - find the best, emerging talent in your town, area, or venue and make yourself indispensable to them. If you are in any doubt about this strategy, then I want to assure you it works - this is exactly how I started in the live concert production industry. I started out by helping fellow local musicians and the bands I knew from my home town. The work was hard, and I was not that well paid, but I had skills that other people needed and, more importantly, I learnt new skills. My career grew from there; I needed to prove my worth before I could progress, but I made the right choices by making myself indispensable to those local music artists. Or, as Max Terlecki (Milo Greene, Transviolet and Borns) said in Billboard, "You just work with a ton of people, doing one-offs until you get referred and a band picks you up"[15]. That is why I recommend this route to a road crew career.

You might be in a band yourself, in which case it will be easy to approach other music artists and bands in your home town, as you probably know them already. If you find out that another artist has secured a great opening slot, or is playing a show out-of-town, then maybe it's time to swallow your pride, put your jealousy to one side, and offer your road crew services to them for the day. "Few roadie jobs require formal credentials, so candidates with limited skills or experience can apply", says Adam Zendel, who has written his doctoral paper on roadie life and working conditions [16]. He adds that there is therefore a 'wide potential labor pool' for road crew work. I disagree with the first statement, and it is true that there is work out there, especially if you get to know the local talent. Brian Forst (Less Than Jake, New Found Glory, Bowling For Soup) is proof of that. He moved to Gainsville, Florida, where he found non-touring work at a record label run by the drummer from Less Than Jake (LTJ). A guitarist himself, he was in an ideal situation when LTJ needed a guitar tech for a string of shows, and since then Brian has gone on to tour full-time [17].

Figure 105: Get to know local talent - the music artists in your town - and make sure they know you.

Build up Your Network.

Do you agree with these statements?

- *'I do not have a network – I'm just starting out in this business'*
- *'I live in the middle of nowhere, there is no network here'*
- *'I am still at school'.*

You may think that you have 'no network' and I disagree with you. Your network is everyone you know – it just happens that some of these people will be more useful in establishing your new career. You would be surprised at the amount of people you already know who can help. Forget about power lunches and business clubs; you have people around you right now who can help you, all you have to do is ask them for advice and help. Still not convinced you have a network? Ask yourself:

- Do you go to shows?
- Do you know people in singers, musicians, or DJs?
- Are you friends with other bands and DJs through social media?
- Do you know people who work in clubs, bars or record store staff?
- Are you a member of clubs and associations at college or university?
- Is your best friend/cousin/neighbour someone in the music business?

If you can answer yes (or maybe) to any of these questions then you have a network, a network that is applicable to what you want to achieve. Your immediate task is to build up this network by spreading the word about your intentions. The result should be that people in your network introduce you to other people, previously unknown to you, that in turn grow your network and will present you with opportunities previously closed to you. Mike Buffa (guitar tech for Maroon 5) has this to say on networking:

"I can't begin to think of how many doors and opportunities have been opened for my career and me just because I went up to someone and talked to them about gear or guitar. It seems so simple and trivial [and] it might not happen when you meet someone, but people know people so be personable and meet as many people as possible."[18]

So, make friends, ask questions, and cause people remember you - for the right reasons.

Use Your Network

Identify what help you need from your network. This could include:

- Finding out which artists from your area are playing shows and letting them know you are available to help.

- Using your network to find the right places to 'advertise' or inform local artists about your freelance services. Is it right or relevant to post notices in local musical instrument shops, rehearsal studios, record stores, and venues., for instance? (figure 205)

- Ensuring your network of venue managers, promoters, rehearsal rooms and music instrument stores know that you are looking to set up a freelance tour crew business.

- Use social media to tell your network what you are up to.

This is stuff you can do, *right now*, regard less of where you live, where you work, or go to school. Once use of your network is to help you keep track of all the national touring acts coming into town. Venue managers and promoters will often give opening slots for those national touring acts to the best local artists. Getting an opening slot for a national touring act can be a big deal for an emerging local artist, and they will obviously want their show to go as well as possible. That local artist will need technical and organisational assistance but may be completely unaware as to how to find it. Therefore, you need to contact those local artists as you hear of their opening gigs and offer your services.

A strategy is to pick at least one of the mid-size venues in your area and make sure you have subscribed to the venue mailing lists, Facebook pages and Twitter feeds that show upcoming concerts. Check to see which local acts (if any) are opening up for the national band. The reality of modern concert touring is that the

Figure 205: Local rehearsal rooms should be part of your network

opening act is often not confirmed until a couple of weeks before the event, leaving you little or no time to offer your services to that band. You therefore need to make sure you have those promising local artists in your network, or that your network can let you know when opening bands have been booked by a local promoter.

The benefit of working for local acts on opening shows is that you may well be able to fit in evening shows around any existing day job. 'Local openers' (as opening acts from your home town are known) are inevitably first on the bill and so will not be expected to load in or sound check until maybe six o'clock in the evening (assuming the standard seven o'clock venue opening time). Then, as they are first on, the local band's performance will be over by eight or nine o'clock which means a relatively early finish for you as well.

Obviously, you will not get paid much (if anything) working with an up-and-coming band. Don't be discouraged through. You must think 'long-term'. This investment of your time and expertise now will be worth more in the bank in the long run. A positive, can-do attitude when dealing with new artists, venue managers and regional booking agents will get you noticed. And getting noticed is your main priority. So, if you are working in a venue as sound, lighting or stage crew make sure you are always, always nice, polite and attentive to the visiting artists – especially local support/opening acts.

Getting Hired by People Outside of Your Network

Presuming your network comes through and you are able to secure work with local artists, it won't be long before one of the artists goes to the next level, taking them with you, or you will want to get national and international work yourself. You should still be using your network for those first recommendations (the acts you are now working with are now part of your network) and you now need to get hired by people working in the wider live music business?

In order to get more tour work, or work from outside your local network, you are going to have to find people who hire touring road crew, and approach them hire you. You need to persuade prospective and existing clients of the need to hire you as opposed to your competitor. This persuasion should always emphasise the features of what you offer and the benefits to your client of using you. This is the selling part; putting across your superior experience, expertise, price, whatever, in order to get the work.

Selling Your Services

In his excellent book, 'Selling Your Services' [19], Robert Bly explains what he calls the 'Five-Step Service Selling Process'.

This involves:

- Generating initial interest in your service.
- Follow up the initial interest to get an appointment or generate a meaningful discussion about your service
- An initial meeting or discussion.
- Getting the assignment or project.
- Keeping the client 'sold' after the sale is made.

I'm going to concentrate on number 1, 'generating initial interest in your service', for most of the rest of this fourth step in the 5-step process.

Initial interest. (a.k.a. marketing)

You are surrounded by messages and information from people trying to get you to have an initial interest in the products or services. These messages take the form of marketing emails, letters, circulars, social media posts, and phone calls, as well as the TV, radio, print, poster and online advertisements you see every day.

You have already read in step 3 that mass advertising of a specialised service, such as a freelance road crew business, is inappropriate. However, you do need to inform potential clients about you and your service. To do this you should use a combination of websites, social media, 'brochures', and résumés.

Business Buyers Have to Buy

Before I get into how you go about creating that initial interest, I should tell you about one very important point that Mr. Bly makes about selling your services: 'business buyers have to buy'. A person looking for a service ultimately has to pick somebody to provide the service - it's not a take-it-or-leave-it proposition; they need that particular service for their business. And, substitute 'artist manager' for business buyer, and you will understand what this means for you - the artist's manager (or band) musthave crew for their next tour. They are 'in the market' i.e. looking for tour crew. This is not an impulse purchase; the manager will be researching the crew personnel available and making a decision. You need to ensure that the manager, 1) knows about you and your service, and 2) becomes interested in using you. Apply the first of Bob Bly's steps, and generate the initial interest in your service, to make this happen.

Initial Interest from Your Own Web Site

I surveyed live music business professionals – booking agents, artist managers and bands –and discovered that 8% of those professionals found their tour crew from internet search (figure 305). This might not sound like a huge amount of people until you consider that Pollstar, a live music business information service, lists more than 2400 artist management and booking companies in the US alone. Using these figures (8% of 2400 people) we can approximate that 200 shows or tours used road crew found directly from searches using Google, (or Bing, perhaps?). That's just for the US, and this figure can only increase as access to the Internet on mobile devices has become easier. Quite simply, you must have your own web site if you want potential clients to find you.

Your Own Website

A website is relatively simple to build and maintain these days (fig 405). There really is no need to learn programming or graphic design in order to have an effective site. 'Effective' is the key word

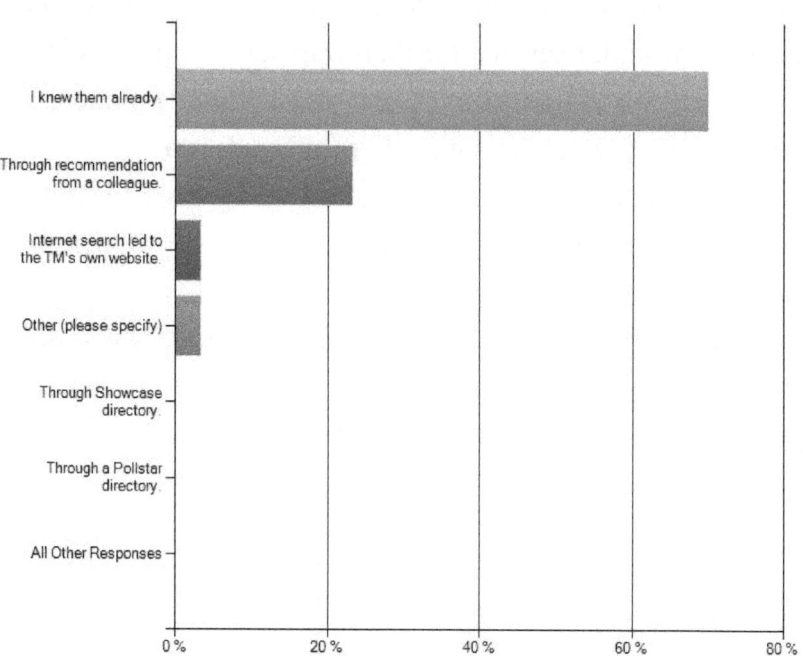

Figure 305: Survey results from the questions, 'where do you find your crew?'

here – your site must appear in the search engines when people are looking and give people who then decide to click through to your site a clear reason for wanting to hire you. A good website can be built in just five steps - so now you have five steps within five steps! Anyway, to build a website you must register a domain, find a web host, design the site, write the content, and optimise the content for the search engines.

Register a Domain

The domain (and domain name) is what people will type in to their browser in order to access your site. Livemusicbusiness.com, for instance, has livemusicbusiness as a domain name and .com as the domain. The domain and name give your site and your business its identity, so choose carefully. You should definitely consider the impact of a *top level domain (TLD)* such as .com

Figure 405: A simple, effective web site

or .co.uk on your business identity; finding good names with the right domain extension is becoming difficult. A whole load of new TLDs have been introduced - including ones that may be perfect for your freelance tour crew business. For instance .engineering (for sound engineers), .company, . services, and many other are now available. So, if your name is Amy Johnson, you could register amyjohnsonsound.engineering, for instance. Registering of domain names is done via the Internet itself – a quick search on Google will turn up the most popular services (figure 505)

Find a Web Host

The web host is a company that stores your online files on their servers and makes your site available on the internet (you can host your own website if you want, but this is technically challenging as well as being very expensive). A good web host will also provide you with a set of controls to make it easier to upload your website documents and design.

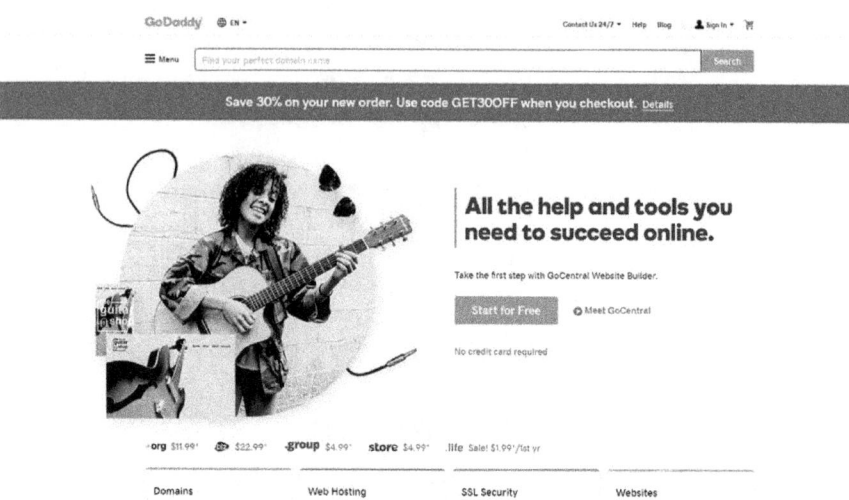

Figure 505: A service offering domain names.

There are many, many web hosting companies these days – again, a search on Google should turn up the most popular providers (figure 605). Don't go for the least expensive offers though. You should check into reliability and 'uptime' scores when comparing web hosts. Uptime is the most important as this is a measure of the total time per month that the host is available on the internet. Look for hosts with uptime scores of as close to 100% as possible. Scores of 90% or less mean your site may not be accessible for 10% of the year - you really don't want your website disappearing for hours or days on end.

Design Your Site

Designing is not only deciding the layout, colours and graphics of your site but should also consider the function and intention of the site. What are you designing your website to do? In your case, as a touring crew person, you need to tell people who arrive at your site:

- who you are

- what you do
- who you have done it for
- what you can do for the visitor
- how much you charge,
- and where they can get hold of you.

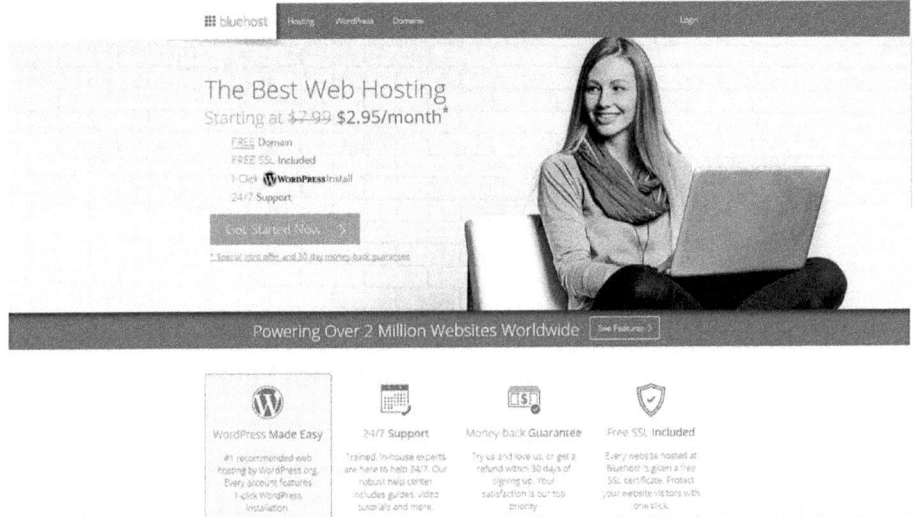

Figure 605: A typical web host service.

This information is more readily given in words than pictures, so I suggest you design a 'brochure' site – one that conveys useful information to your prospective clients, using the language that they are expecting to see. The easiest way to do this is to use blogging software to create your site. Don't worry; I am not expecting you to have to write reams of content or a post to your site every day. Blogs and blogging software create an ideal framework to present information, are easy to set up and most are free.

Wordpress is the most popular and flexible blogging software and comes in two versions. The hosted version at www.wordpress.com (figure 705) means you can set up a simple brochure site with a couple of pages of information, your résumé and contact

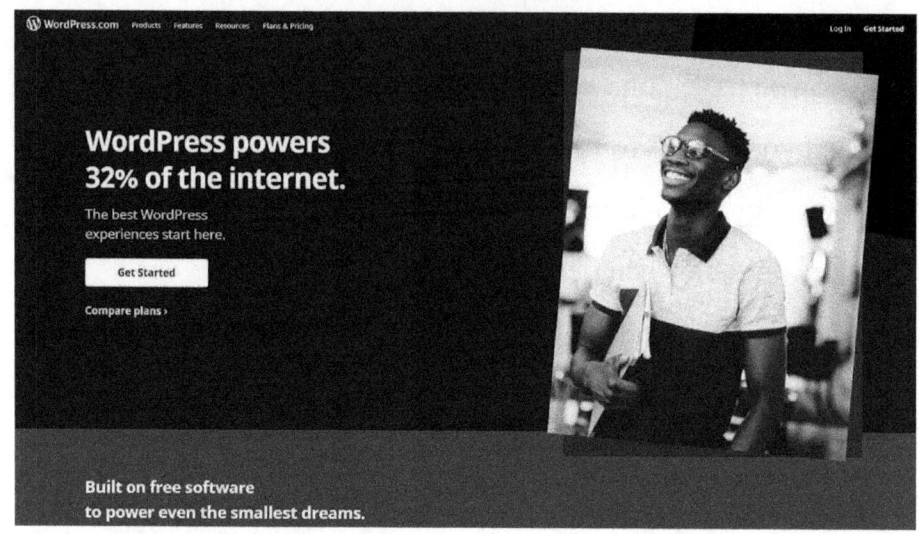

Figure 705: Wordpress.com - hosted for you and has some limitations for future growth.

details in a couple of minutes. For more advanced functionality, such as being able to completely customise the look of your site, you should check out a self-hosted Wordpress installation, using the free software from wordpress.org (figure 805). 60 million web sites use the self-hosted Wordpress, and I thoroughly recommend it. (www.livemusicbusiness.com uses Wordpress!). Whichever you choose, you will find that you can design the site fairy quickly and easily, adding any logos, pictures and text needed to sell yourself and your services to potential clients.

Content and Search Engine Optimisation

You need to create great, relevant content for your site and, as I mentioned before, it's all about the words. Your prospective clients will use Google (does anybody use anything else?) to find touring crew - which is a 'search engine'. Search engines still look at the words on a website to determine how useful or relevant a site is to the needs of the person searching (search engines cannot search pictures yet - only words associated with pictures). You must write

Figure 805: Wordpress. org - slightly harder to set up, and flexible and less expensive in the long term.

content containing words that are relevant to what your potential clients are looking for, I.e. 'live sound engineer', or 'concert tour manager'. This process of writing relevant words and sentences is called 'search engine optimisation' (SEO) and, done well, will help your website get found when people search for touring road crew for their tour or event.

Let's see an example in action. Say I need an FOH engineer for a tour with a band that is based in London, England. I go to Google and search 'FOH engineer london'. They are my 'search terms'. I enter them into Google and a list of results is displayed. This page of results is called the 'search engine results page' or SERPs .Now, I don't know about you, but I very rarely go beyond page one of the results shown on Google, and so your aim therefore is to create a website, with relevant content, site title and other information, that will appear on the first page of the SERPs

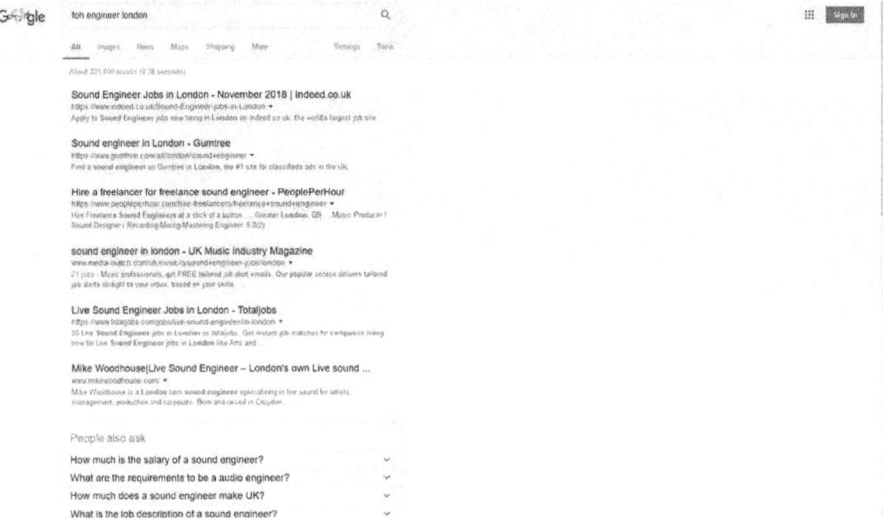

Figure 905: The 'search engine results pages' (SERPs) for my search terms 'FOH engineer london'.

Figure 905 shows that some of these results are irrelevant to me - its just that Google has found lots of content on these sites that about 'foh engineer london' and so thinks that I may be interested in them. I am not, but I am interested in this entry here highlighted in figure 1005:

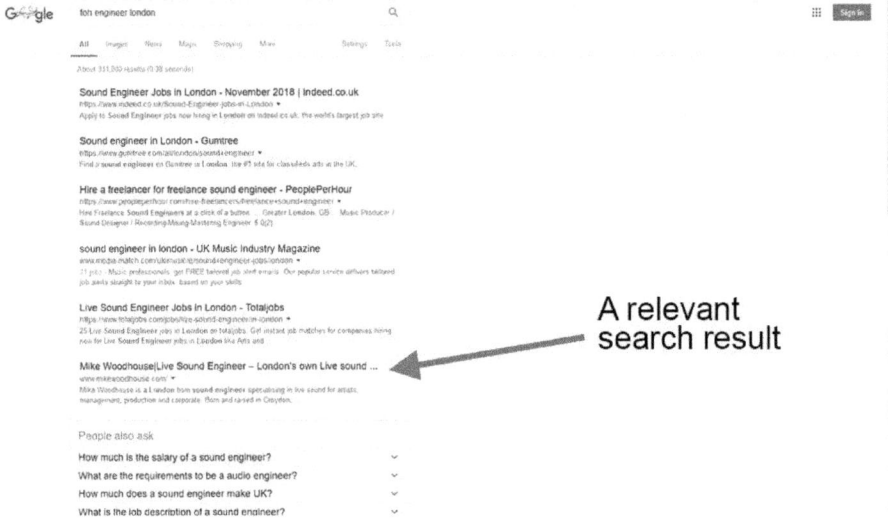

Figure 1005: This result looks relevant to my search for 'FOH engineer london'.

Figure 1005 shows that the site tile and description are both relevant to what I need, and so I am very likely to click on here to explore as to whether Mike Woodhouse is the person I want to hire for my tour or event. When I click through (fig1105), and again (fig1205), I see that Mike may be perfect for what I need.

Figure 1105: Clicking through on the results shows this...

Figure 1205: And this. Mike looks perfect for what I need.

From the example, you can see that Mike has used relevant words as part of his SEO. His page uses 'live sound engineer', London' 'FOH' etc, in his description and page title. Google has looked at these words and sentences and decided that this page is relevant to what I am looking for. You should also note that there only two listings for FOH engineers on this first page - clearly there is an opportunity here!

SEO is not difficult and most of it is common sense. There are activities and practices you should avoid though, otherwise you may get yourself 'banned' from the Google search results - which kind of defeats the object! I therefore recommend you do some extra research on creating your web site and optimising it for search. The best way of doing this is to read up or take an online course; Google itself offers their own online learning and certificate in SEO. Search, 'digital garage' to see their course.

Your Site Content for Human Beings

SEO is important, and your site also needs to be relevant to real, live human beings once they click on it - not just a bunch of words designed to lure the search engines. I look at the very few crew web sites I see online and try to put myself in the mind of someone who is looking for crew to hire when studying them. The following is a list of the things that I think are useful for someone looking for crew (and will show up in the search engine results pages):

- Description of what you do – for example 'backline tech', 'FOH engineer', 'rigger'.

- A relevant and up-to-date list of the clients, bands and tours you have for/on

- Any relevant training, awards or degrees.

- What are you doing right now — for example 'Available for tours until March 31st' or 'On tour in Europe until April 2019".

- Testimonials (these are extremely important and there will be more on this later)

- Relevant contact information – you mobile/cellular number, email address, and social media pages.

To avoid getting lots of spam, you should disguise your email address such as this: andyDOTreynolds{AT}livemusicDONT-WRITETHISBITbusinessDOTcom, or use a contact form. Self-hosted sites using Wordpress can use the excellent 'Contact Form 7' to allow clients to contact you (figure 1305).

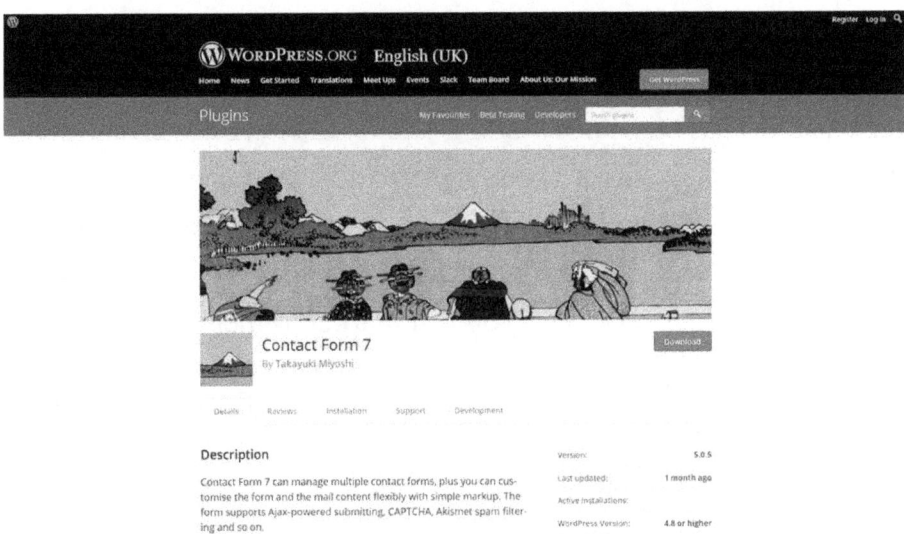

Figure 1305: Contact Form 7 for self-hosted Wordpress sites will help cut down spam emails sent via your web site.

Whatever you decide to include on your site, update it regularly (which is easy using blogging software such as Wordpress). The first contact a potential client has with you will almost certainly be through your web site – make sure that client knows exactly who you are, what you do and what you are doing now. There are very few road crew professionals using their own web site to attract and inform new clients and this is a brand-new opportunity that you can take advantage of.

Initial Interest Using Email Marketing

The only problem with attracting visitors to your site is that they can do just that - visit. The person searching may not like your site, not be 100% interested in what your site offers or become distracted; in all these cases they will take a quick look at your page go elsewhere. You have no idea who they were, what they needed or if they found your site even remotely interesting and useful. You therefore need some way of finding out who your visitors are, gauging their reactions to your site and, if they are interested but had to go away, have some way of contacting them in the future. Presently there is no automatic, inexpensive or easy way to know the exact details of who is visiting your web site, but you can set up a process to capture a visitor's email address fairly easily. You can then use this email address (and other information you can capture) to contact the person and gauge their initial interest in your site and your services - you can market to them using email.

Email marketing is still extremely powerful - 72% of companies say they prefer to receive emails[20], rather than post, telephone calls or social media, and so it makes sense for you to use it as part of your gauging initial interest in your freelance road crew business.

Email marketing usually consists of three activities - offering a 'lead magnet' - a free report, 'how-to' guide, copy of your resume, something else of value to the potential customer that you can give away for free, asking the person to give you their name and email address in exchange for the lead magnet, and then contacting the person either automatically or via individual messages after they have received the lead magnet. All three activities can be automated using software and there are numerous books and courses that deal with email marketing so again, do some research and read up on how to start your email marketing practises.

How to get New Contact Email Addresses

The traditional method of persuading a visitor to give up their email address for something of value - a free report or white paper - is not applicable to you when trying to gain initial interest from clients. An artist manager who has come to your website is not really interested in anything else, other than whether you are the right person to hire for a forthcoming tour or event. She is not really interested in your 'free gift'. So, instead, why don't you offer her a PDF of your résumé that includes all your experience, and skills, along with your current rate-card. You can include this, with a simple 'Download my résumé and rate card here' button, somewhere prominent on your website. When the client clicks the button, you have a simple form that says, 'I'd like to add you to my database of music business professionals - please enter your email address and name here'. (There are numerous books, guides and software that will help you automate this process, as I mentioned before.)

Having this type of email 'opt-in', as it's called, will give your client information about you, which she wanted, and give *you* the contact details of another new potential client, which is what you wanted. Then it is a matter of seeing who has given you their information by logging into your email collection system every couple of days and perhaps 'googling' (searching online) the names and email addresses you see there. Make a note of the acts, singers and DJs the new contacts represent and enter them into a spreadsheet. Then, when contacting each manager, you can mention the acts they represent, which will show you know about that manager, and their business.

The beauty of having a contact from, and your resume and rate card as a 'lead magnet' is that the process is automated. Clients will find you, if your web page is optimised properly, and only the clients who are really interested will contact you, or download the lead magnet. You then have their contact info, in both cases, and can answer their question (if from the contact from) or drop them a polite email to offer solutions to their problem. They have come to you though- you did not have to search for them!

As well as setting up this kind of automated system, you may feel the need to search out for some additional contacts. A quick Google around of music management companies and booking agents may prove frustrating though, as names and email addresses are not readily provided on these sites - probably so the owners and employees are not inundated with emails from young artists, and their mothers! You need to find some contacts though, and you could buy one of the music business trade directories, such as the directory from Pollstar (figure 1405), and they can be expensive. I therefore recommend Hunter (hunter.io), a browser extension which will find (and suggest) relevant email addresses and other contact information for any given website.

Say you wanted to find a contact at Red Light Management - managers of Dave Matthews Band, Bastille, Luke Bryan, Alabama Shakes, Chris Stapleton, Odesza, and Phish, amongst many others. You would first go to the Red Light Management website (www.redlightmanagement.com) and, having installed the Hunter extension from the Play Store (play.google.com), you would click on the Hunter icon in the toolbar. You can see the

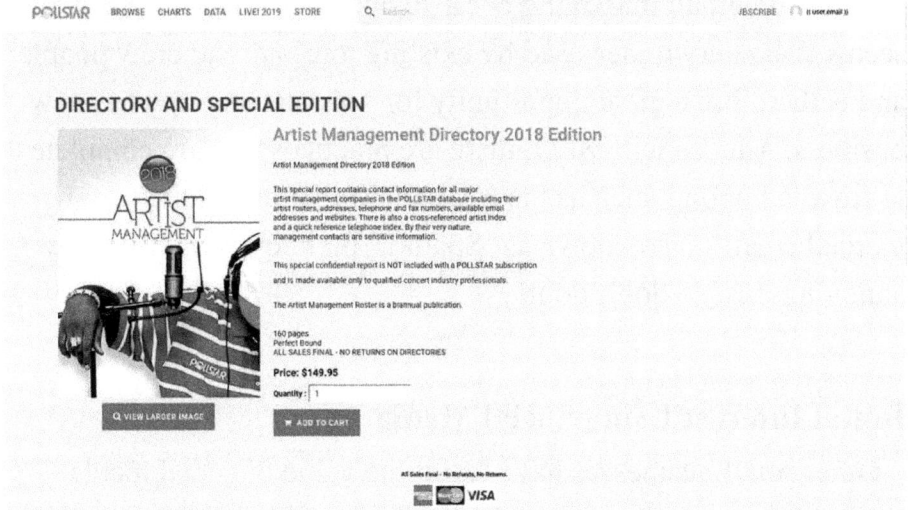

Figure 1405: The Pollstar Artist Management directory. Expensive and useful.

pop up box that would then result, displaying a list of associated email addresses (figure 1406). This is the basic functionality of Hunter - registering for a (free) account gives increasingly relevant results.

Figure 1406: Hunter.io can be used to find email addresses from artist management and booking agency websites.

mention email marketing because, like web sites and SEO, it has to be very under-used by existing touring road crew people, and is therefore a great opportunity for you, starting up your new business. And, as with SEO, there are practices that are completely frowned upon - such as the bulk sending of unsolicited commercial email - also known as 'Spam'. You know what it is, how annoying it is, so don't do it!

Initial Interest Using Social Media

Other small businesses have learnt the value of social media (SM) - Facebook, Twitter, LinkedIn, Instagram and (to a certain extent) YouTube - to find and keep customers and you should do the same. Currently, Facebook and LinkedIn are the two most important networks for small business marketing - some 52% of business surveyed use Facebook to find and keep new customers [21].

You probably have a Twitter or Facebook profile already. Your profile on these services should now reflect the new, professional nature of what you are offering as a freelance tour crew business, and not that of your personal life. If your page is currently focused on the more personal elements of your life (your favourite amusing videos or posts about kayaking for instance) then either remove those elements or, in the case of Facebook, Twitter, and Instagram, start a new business-based profile.

Starting a new profile is as easy as when you created your original profile - and free. Your goal in creating new profiles is to present a unified, professional looking, set of places where prospective clients can find out about you. Remember, everyone has preferences - some people may not use Twitter and prefer Facebook for instance. You must have a presence on the major platforms to cater to most potential clients. I would say today that that means Facebook, Twitter, Instagram and LinkedIn. You can see examples of a unified, professional approach by looking at my various social media sites. You will notice I have created the same look and feel across all the sites - anyone clicking around will recognise certain elements - the logo and images, for instance, and be hopefully left with an impression of professionalism.

How to Create Business Profiles

Each of the social networks have pretty good guides on how to create business-type profiles. Depending on the specific platform, you will probably need a personal account first, after that you simply create the business page or profile by following their instructions. Once you have created a business profile in, say, Facebook, you should spend some time optimising the profile. Optimising in this case means uploading the pictures and graphics that set your profile apart, filling out the necessary information, such as what your business does, and your preferred way of being contacted.

Getting the look and feel of your new profile is not hard, even if you have no graphic design skills. I thoroughly recommend Canva to create the kinds of logos and graphics you see on my sites (figure 1605). Canva is online and is free (as in beer) for most of the stiff you need to do with it. You can set a size for the graphic you need to create, then simply drag, drop, resize and colour all the elements and text you need in order to create the graphics and logos for your SM network profiles. Canva even has pre-sized examples of most of the popular SM network graphics - Facebook headers for instance - that you can customise easily and quickly. All the SM sites require different sizes for their graphics and you can find out what the various sizes are here:

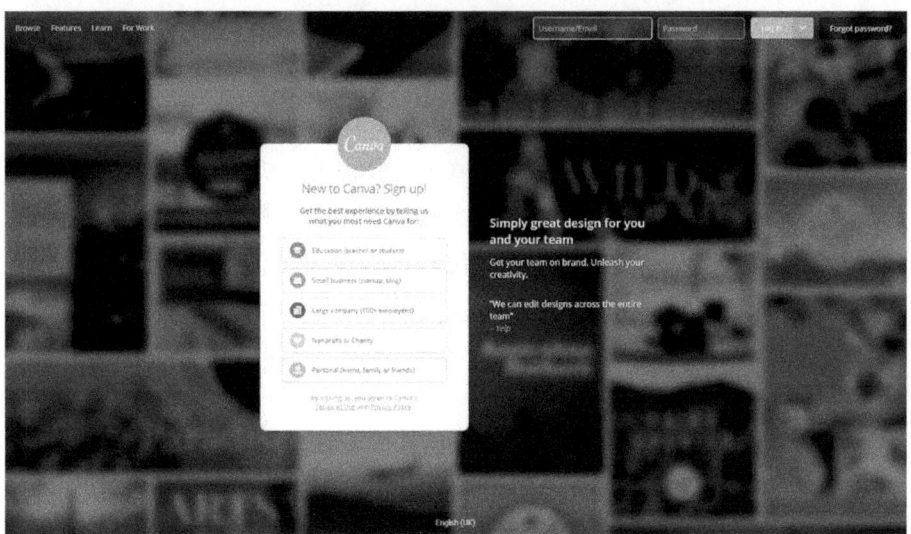

Figure 1605: Canva is a free online tool for creating graphics and logos.

(cont.) http://pegfitzpatrick. com/quick-tips-for-great-social-media-graphics/. Then simply go into Canva and set the dimensions of a new design according to the suggestions from Peg on her site.

What to Post

Social media is like email - a fantastic communication tools and totally open to abuse by unscrupulous people. The idea of social networks is just that - a network. Once you have got people in your network you should treat them with equal respect and be careful of how you interact with them - sending 20 tweets a day saying, 'hire me for you tour' is going to annoy everyone who follows you and will make them quickly unfollow you! Instead, you should use your social media networks to keep yourself in people's minds, along with occasional posts or tweets that ask or tell your network about your work. Now the different social networks are used for different things - Facebook can be used to tell long stories, Twitter for short news about your opinions or moods, and Instagram for striking images with an unusual message, for instance.

Say you are have some work with a band at a gig, tour or event and you want to use SM to build , and inform, your network. You should:

- Follow the band, manager and record company on Twitter, Facebook and Instagram
- Re-tweet their relevant tweets i.e. tweets about any of the gigs you are working on.
- Like their relevant posts on Instagram
- Like their relevant posts on Facebook - maybe add a positive comment as well.

Then send a tweet on each show day, including the promoters, venue and band's @handle, as well as the cities #hashtag. For example, ' A lovely day here in #denver, just loading into @reallygreatvenue with @nameofband. Hope its a great show with @nameofpromoter' (figure 1705). The idea behind this is that the band, promoter and venue will then re-tweet you message, which will reach all their followers. Other managers, bands and booking agents may follow the original sender, in which case you have reached them and may be followed by them. You should also re-tweet and comment on as many of the tweets and posts after each show - especially if the tweets and posts mention the sound or lights, or anything else that you were responsible for during the show. Lighting engineers have an advantage here - Instagram pictures of shows will feature your work - the lights - and you can post those pictures, adding the comment 'My lighting design' or' really proud of my work with the lights last night'.

Figure 1705: An example of the type of Twitter message you can post - including all the people you have helped get you this work.

Another example of using SM would be towards the end of the tour, where you should also post about being available for work, but not in an obvious way. 'Two days until ~endlesstour with @ nameofband finishes - whats next, I wonder?' is an example. This tye of post will alert your network, who should hopefully include you clients, that you will be available soon. You never know, they might just have been in the process of looking for new tour crew...

LinkedIn

You should have a look at LinkedIn as part of your social media strategy (figure 1805). LinkedIn is primarily a business networking and job finding site and has, in recent years, added other social media functions in order to appeal to more users. However, most people still use it to either find jobs or find people in companies that they want to do business with. The live music production business is not really a great user of LinkedIn, but many of the artist managers and booking agents do have profiles, and they are the people who may be giving you paid work. It is probably worth you also then having a profile on LinkedIn, and adding these

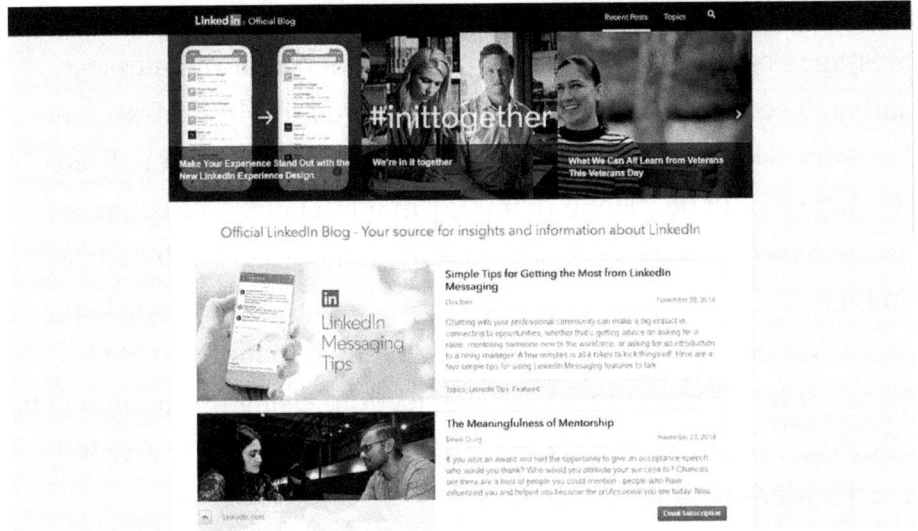

Figure 1805: LinkedIn can be very useful in finding new and ongoing work and has to be used properly for you to benefit.

people as connections. This is a simple process and it will take time to do properly.

For example, let's say you're looking for artist managers that you want to contact to expand your client list. Here's the procedure you'd follow: Type 'artist manager' into the top search bar on LinkedIn. You will then see a list of results. You can then filter these results, say by size of company of city, for instance. When you have a list of artist managers you are happy with, you should go through them all and make sure that each of the possible contacts has an active profile showing. This means looking at their profile and seeing if they have uploaded a picture, have filled in more than a couple of the fields, have some other connections listed, and so on and so forth. A person with a standard, 'unpopulated' profile probably does not use LinkedIn that often, and therefore is not going to be worth trying to add to your contacts on this platform. So, assuming your chosen potential contacts have an active profile, you need to invite them to connect with you on LinkedIn. You do this by clicking on the 'connect' button and filling in the field that LinkedIn then presents to you. Filling in the field for the message is important - you should send a personalised message and not use the default, 'I'd Like to Add you to My Professional Network on LinkedIn', message. An example of a personalised message would be, 'Hello (name), I'm a freelance live sound engineer based in New York. I am a huge fan of (band you manage) and I'd like to add you to my live music business contacts here on LinkedIn". You are not trying to get them to hire you at this stage - it really is just making a connection. Using this approach is effective - about 50 - 75% of people you contact in this way will accept your invitation.[22]

You may find that the person you are trying to connect with needs you to know their email address before you can connect on LinkedIn. This is not a massive problem as you can probably find their address using Hunter (see 'Initial interest using email marketing' above), or via a trade directory if you can afford to buy one. When a person accepts your invitation they are added to your connections in LinkedIn. You can now contact them, through LinkedIn, in a fairly similar way to how you would through a direct message on other social media platforms (I would also ask your new contact for their email address so you can contact them outside of LinkedIn). As with other SM, you should not abuse your relationship with your LinkedIn network by constantly messaging and harassing those people who have connected with you. Rather, you should contact them at relevant times. A good example of this is to remind people you may be available for work for an upcoming season, say the summer festivals or the busy winter holiday season. In the case of summer festivals, you may want to contact artist managers in January or February, just saying something along these lines: 'Hello (name). I'm sure you are booking (name of managers acts) onto festivals bills for this summer and so just letting you know I am available during that time if I can help with tour management (or sound engineering, or whatever your actual skill is).'

LinkedIn is an invaluable resource if used with care and tact. There are some excellent guides and books available and I would spend some time researching in order to buy one and make the most of this business tool.

Managing your Social Networks.

Its great having these forms of communication at your fingertips and, as with everything else, there is a danger that sending out messages and keeping on top of your growing network will become too time-consuming. Certainly, composing and posting to the four social networks you have examined (plus the others) in this step will take some time, especially if you are a regular poster. Luckily there are services that help you to compose and post to all your SM at the same time - and you can even schedule longer posts on Facebook for instance, in advance. I recommend you sign up for one of these services, as they will help you to run a more effective SM 'campaign', and save you quite a bit of time as well. Two such services are Buffer and Hootsuite (figure 1905), and there are others. Have a look around and see which one offers what you need.

'Brochures'

I have put the word 'brochures' in inverted commas as I am referring to any kind of sales material – flyer, rate card, brochure, pamphlet, letter or PDF – that you send to a potential client who asks for further information.

Figure 1905: Services such as Buffer and Hootsuite (pictured) help to organise and schedule posts to your SM network.

It used to be that the only way to learn more about a company was to ask for a physical brochure. After seeing or hearing an advert, you would call that company or fill in a mail-in card and the sales materials would be sent to you. Today, increased access to information via the Internet has diminished the importance of such materials - yet they are still a very useful thing to thing to send. Not only do brochures provide that little extra personal service to a potential client, they act as an indicator to the amount and type of clients interested in your service. Say a client calls or emails you saying she heard about you via a colleague and wants some more information. You send her your standard sales material (whatever that may be, more on this later). By doing this, you have taken two important steps towards getting more work. Firstly, you have given a potential client the information she needed, which may or may not answer her questions and prompt her to hire you. Secondly, and perhaps more importantly, you now have the contact details of a new client. Even if she does not hire you this time around you have her details and can call, email or 'direct message' her (using a social media service) as part of a marketing campaign in the future. Brochures, either physical or digital, help to 'pre-qualify' your clients — the ones who are really interested in you are easier to contact (they asked you for information) and are more likely to hire you.

Physical Brochures

An example of a physical brochure is a single-page two-sided letter, printed on high-quality, thicker paper. The letter can then be posted, along with a business card. As this is often a response to a request for information, your letter should contain extra information to that already listed on your web site. The benefits of your service, common problems the client may have (that you can help solve) and detailed pricing information could all be included in your brochure letter.

Sending brochures is old-fashioned though, and these days usually only the activity of very large companies who can afford to print and post physical brochures. For you, at this stage in your new company, sending your brochures as PDF emails attachments is a better bet

Digital Brochures

All of your on line activity - your website and your social media sites, posts and tweets - are 'brochures' in the purest sense of the word; they are pictures and words containing information that will market your business. However, the online version of the physical brochure is easier to create and distribute, and therefore the form that is most common. Brochures now take the form of a PDF sales letter or booklet, which does the same job of telling the person requesting the information all about you and your business. They can be used as a response to a request for information, and as a 'lead magnet' - as described in the lesson on email marketing. Digital brochures are extremely useful and well worth spending some time to write and create.

Making a Digital Brochure

Creating a digital brochure is a fairly simple process of two parts. First, you must write what you want to include in the brochure (the 'copy'), and then format the words, perhaps including pictures, to create a pleasant-looking PDF that can be sent to potential clients.

The Copy

I have previously mentioned Robert Bly, and I'm going to turn to him again for inspiration on copywriting. Mr Bly is a professional copywriter, and he offers these headings as a start for your brochure (remember, your website is also a brochure, and the following are a great way of sub-divide information about you and your service on your site):

- Who I Am
- What I Do
- Who /I Work For - list of bands, artists, and managers you have worked for so far
- When You Should Call Me (And When You Shouldn't)
- Why My Service Is Successful for Our Clients - a description of a problem solved, benefits of being local. Inexpensive or some training that s useful
- How My Service Works
- The Next Step - a contact form, phone number or some other

way the prospective client can ask about your availability. Perhaps an email sign-up form as examined in the lesson on email marketing?[23]

The Design

You were introduced to Canva, the online graphic design tool, in lesson 5 of this step. You can also use Canva to design the complete brochure, and export it as a PDF that can be emailed or used as a lead magnet, or as a printable version should you decide to spend money on printing and mailing. Canva comes with templates for US letter and A4 brochures, all you have to do it add graphics, backgrounds and write headlines and copy until your heart (and eye) is content. Some elements that Canva suggest will cost money (currently $1 each) and there are thousands of free images, backgrounds and fonts to choose from as well. Canva is so ridiculously easy to use there is no point me explaining further, just head over to Canva.com and play around with it for yourself. After this finish reading this step, of course!

Résumés

You may be wondering, as a person running a business, why you would send out a résumé? Surely résumés are used by people looking for jobs? Well, you may run your own freelance tour crew business, but a résumé is still a very useful tool. 80% of music industry professionals that I surveyed expect to see a résumé from a potential crew person; it is still the accepted way of receiving information about someone and, even if you are using brochures and lead magnets, you should still have a well-prepared résumé available for clients who may request one. However, because you are using your résumé to enhance information your client may have already, you need to make sure your résumé is in the correct format.

Chronological Résumé

Figure 2005 shows a chronological résumé. As you can see the résumé lists the persons career/job achievements with the most recent at the top. Chronological résumés are the most common form of résumé I see and, for the live music industry, the most inappropriate. Your résumé is a marketing message just like your web site and mail outs and the information it contains needs to be relevant and concise. For example, your music industry client does not need to know about the four months you spent working in a coffee house or that you studied marketing at college. Instead you should highlight only the training, experience and an aspiration that is relevant to the client's needs – that of finding suitable tour crew. Chronological résumés are especially problematic when you are just starting out as live production service provider, as you do not have that many tours or shows to list on the résumés. Listing every day job and part time position you have held may show you are a diligent worker, but tells your client nothing that will convince her you have the skills and experience to solve her problem, which is finding experienced show crew for her tour or event.

Functional Résumé

A functional résumé, such as the one shown in figure 2105, will highlight your suitability to a client, and this is the type you should send. The functional résumé works for you as it only lists the relevant parts of your work history to date. And if you don't have a relevant work history then the functional résumé will still

Rhoda Crew

16 Arcadian Road, Boxley, Kent AD1 1AA
D.O.B 15/10/84
Home Tel: 020 3038
Mobile Tel: 07972 243

rhodcrew@yahoo.com

WORK EXPERIENCE

- **National Accounts Co-ordinator** *Mega Music, London*
September 2016 to April 2019
  - Produced Sales department release and competitor schedules
  - Point of contact for all Sales department enquiries
  - Managed single and album sales notes for distribution
  - Approved and supplied artwork for adverts
  - Ordered promos, watermarks and DVDs for distribution

Sales and New Media *CIA Records, London*
July 2011 to September 2016
- Produced all Sales department schedules and midweek reports
- Point of contact for all Sales department enquiries
- Managed single and album sales notes for distribution
- Sent out relevant artwork and advertising tagging to label accounts
- General admin duties including taking minutes, ordering promotional material etc

Creative Department *Worldwide Music, London*
April 2009 to June 2011
- Liaising with photographers, stylist, managers, editing suites and directors in order to meet deadlines for photo shoots and video sessions
- Re-cataloguing archived material
- Booking couriers and transportation

Artist Relations *Bag on Your Head Records, London*
February 2002 to April 2009
- Responsible for producing artist schedules i.e. TV, radio, booking hotels and flights etc
- Event management and venue sourcing for artists
- Liaising with TV and radio pluggers in order to produce artist promotion schedule
- Managed ticket requests including festivals and award events
- Invoicing, raising purchase orders, and organising artists transport/ couriers
- Responsible for buying gifts for artists

Label Assistant (Work Experience Placement) *Aalto Records, London*
February 2001 to January 2002
- Finding and booking venues for band tours negotiating band payment, support acts, and stage times.
- Responsible for listening & reviewing artists demos
- Point of contact for label enquiries
- Produced promotional singles for distribution to media outlets
- Attended gigs on behalf of the label with the intention of finding new talent

Figure 2005: A Chronological résumé. This type of résumé may not be appropriate for you if you have little relevant experience in concert touring.

show a potential client that you are focused and willing to learn. The 'Job objective' section is the place to state that you are inexperienced in this area but are willing to learn. 'To secure an entry-level stage hand position on domestic and international tours' is an example of a good job objective. It shows you are realistic about your experiences ('level-entry') and the scope of your work ('domestic and international').

Rhoda Managere

Flat 4 Duchess Street, London, ES1 999
Mobile: +44 (0)776 68 • e-mail: rhodmanager@aol.com

Job Objective.
To become an internationally recognised **tour and production manager** in the live music industry.

Qualifications

- Tour manager responsible for advancing all aspects of a tour (both national and international) including transport, accommodation, budgeting, hiring personnel, creating schedules, technical requirements of sound, lights and staging for performers including Millions Of Americans and First Name Last Name.

- Tour production responsible for advancing all aspects of a tour production including transport, budgeting, hiring personnel, creating schedules, technical requirements of sound, lights and staging for performers including Millions Of Americans and First Name Last Name.

- Company manager responsible for setting up and running tours.

Professional Skills

- Technical skills include sound engineering (CVE), lighting design and backline technician.
- Full UK and European driving liscence
- National Rigging Certificate
- MS Office

EDUCATION / QUALIFICATION

1979	BA hons English and Drama, London University
1976	3 A-Levels English, Economics and Geography
1974	7 O-Leves including Maths and English

PERSONAL

Date of Birth: 11th November 1997   Nationality: British

Figure 2105: A functional résumé that highlights what you are good at, and what you aim to achieve.

Step 5: Do A Good Job and Get More Road Crew Work

Having gained a foothold in the live music business, you will want to get more work and grow your business. And competition for touring work can be fierce, even given the comparatively small amount of road crew professionals. Your primary focus therefore is to always do the best job that you can. You need to be punctual, reliable, contentious and sober when working, and foster a 'can-do' attitude, both for yourself and for the band and crew you are working alongside. You can still apply all the strategies outlined in step 4 to further your road crew career, and these will undoubtedly help you to get more work. Success will come, in small steps at first, and it won't be long until you are booked for months in advance. And, as you grow and expand, taking on ever longer and more lucrative tours, you should always try to keep your eye on the day-to-day operations of your business. You may be away for weeks, or even months at a time, and you don't want problems piling up while you are gone. Read on to find out how to make sure that your business continues to grow - and that there are no surprises that could cause your business to fail.

Clients and Invoicing

I made some terrible mistakes when I started touring, especially when it came to get paid! I really did not understand how it all worked, and had no idea about how much to charge, who was paying me and how to send an invoice. I nearly went broke a couple of time, after sending invoices to the wrong people and not getting paid until a couple of month later. I read up about standard business practises though and I subsequently learnt that I always need to do four things in order to get paid promptly: check my client, agree the terms of service, set a payment schedule, and plan ahead.

Check Your Client.

You may be offered a road crew job by a booking agent, artist manager, or business manager. However, these people do not actually pay your invoice. In nearly all cases, your salary as road crew is paid by the artist, either from their own vast cash reserves (if they are U2 or Major Lazer for instance) or, more likely, from record company tour support - which you examined in step 1.

One of your first tasks after being offered employment on a tour is to find out whom exactly is paying you. You need to approach this tactfully, as you don't want to come across as being 'all-business' or mistrustful. But you must ask the person who hires you about the invoicing details as part of the initial discussions.

Invoices are made out to a specific company or business entity and, in the case of road crew touring work, this may take the form of 'Xxx Touring LLC' (where xxx is the name of the artist), or 'Xxx record label.' Artists will set up a company (as you have done) to administer the finances of their touring - usually a LLC if it is band, and this company will be looked after by their business management. Ask the artist manager to give you the details of the touring company. When you have these invoicing details, you should find a real, live person in the relevant business management or record company accounting or accounts payable office. Call that person (don't email them as they can/will ignore your message) to let him or her know who you are and what your role is and tell that person to expect an invoice from you. Ask whether you need a 'purchase order' (PO) or other reference. Large organisations, such as major record companies, do not often accept invoices for purchases that have not been authorised; they will require you to be on their supplier list before they will accept an invoice from you, and will give you a PO number when you have been 'approved' as a supplier. Most record companies use a web-based portal to do this; figure 106 shows the supplier portal for Universal Music, for instance.

Becoming a supplier can be a long process involving filling out some forms, usually via a portal such as Uniport, and waiting - sometimes up to four weeks. You cannot send an invoice until the forms have been filled in, checked and you have been added to the system as a recognised supplier to the record company. You will then be issued a PO so that you can send in an approved invoice. Please remember this fact if you do any work where you are being paid directly by a record company - it can take months for the necessary paperwork to be completed, your PO issued and your invoice to be paid. This can have a massive effect on your cash flow. You will not need to become a supplier for most of the work you do for touring artists, and it is something you should be aware of.

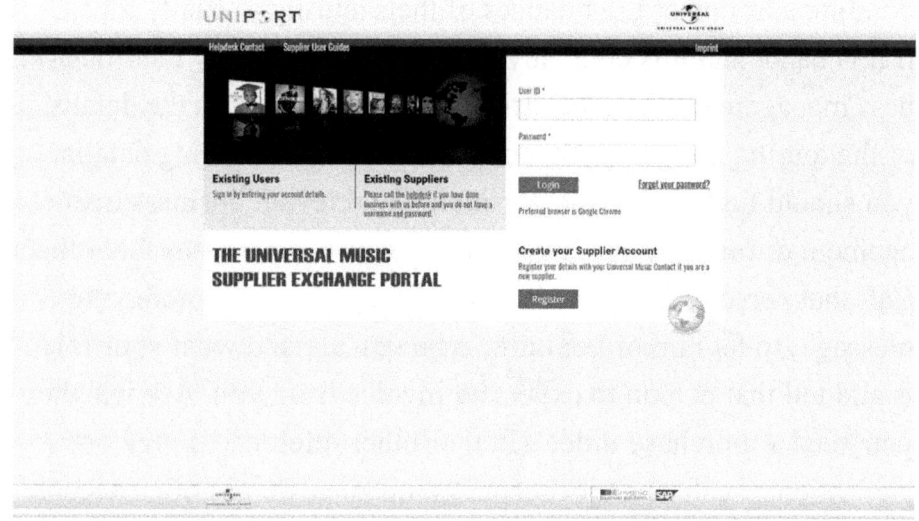

Figure 106: Universal Records' Uniport - their supplier payment portal.

Agree the Terms of Service

After establishing the invoicing details with whoever has hired you, the next step is to negotiate the details of the services you are going to provide on the tour. Again, this is standard business practice so don't feel awkward or that you are being pushy in setting these terms.

The trouble with working on-the-road is that there is always so much to do on each show day, and the spirit of the 'show must go on' means you end up working for longer and on more tasks than you would expect. Which is fine, as the work should be fun, and you are part of a creative process. At the same time, you don't want to get tired and burnt out, or be put in a position where your clients (the artist or whoever) expect you just to do whatever is asked. It's a good idea therefore to set your terms of service before the tour or event commences. These could include what you see as your duties, what those duties involve and, more importantly, what you will not do, unless it is agreed in writing beforehand

and/or you can charge extra. So, let's use the example of an audio engineer. The services the engineer may set out might include the following duties and exceptions:

Duties:

- Setting up of FOH mixing equipment
- Setting up, positioning and cabling of stage microphones
- Completing sound check procedure to artists satisfaction, to take no more than 1 hour from commencement of artist commencing full band run-through
- Mixing of FOH sound for artist performance
- Packing up and break down of relevant FOH equipment
- Other duties relevant to FOH engineering to artists satisfaction

Exceptions:

- Load in, set up, maintenance, tear down and load out of artists back line equipment
- Attendance of sound checks lasting more than one hour from commencement of artist full band run-through
- Mixing of FOH for support/opening bands
- Operation of stage monitoring, except if stage monitoring is operated from FOH console
- Set up, sound check and mixing of two or more shows in any 24-hour period (for instance in-store, TV/radio/internet promo, after-show etc.)

This is an example, and you get the idea. The sound engineer has specified what tasks she is comfortable undertaking each day for the money, and what tasks and activities she won't do. The client may subsequently ask the engineer to help with setting up the back line (for instance), and the engineer can decline, as it is stipulated in the service agreement that she won't touch back line, or she can ask for more money. In either case, everything is clear and not open to any misunderstanding. The services you agree to provide can be incorporated into a document, that also sets out the agreed salary or rate for the work, along with a payment schedule. Which brings me onto...

Set a Payment Schedule

Insist on a portion of your salary be paid to you before the tour starts. Getting a portion of the money up front will help your cash flow and shows commitment from the artist's business team. Likewise, if the tour is going to last for a month or more, insist on being paid weekly for the duration of the tour. You can't really afford to work for three months without any income from the tour, and then must wait another thirty days once the tour has finished to get paid. Running a business is all about cash flow, so agree on a payment schedule that is going to help you avoid cash flow problems. Ideally you want a third of the total tour salary up front, another third half way through the tour, and the final third within 10 days of the tour finishing. The good news is that, in my experience, many artist's business management companies will set you up on the artist company's payroll, ensuring weekly salary payments into your account.

Plan Ahead

Getting paid on time is half the battle - you also need to ensure you have work starting directly after you finish your present tour. Plan to anticipate when you will be working and get paid again. Tours and events are booked four to eight months in advance; once you finish on one tour it may take you a couple of weeks to find and be hired onto another tour (if you can be hired at all). The new tour then may then not be going out for another 1-2 months. You are therefore looking at 2 to 5 months without work. Will the pay check from your last tour last that long?

Rates of Pay

Economics in general, and that of the touring market, have not really supported an increase in pay amounts to tour crew in the last 30 years. Unfortunately, there is no international standard pay scale for touring road crew. Artists pay what they can afford, and the lack of record company support for some artist means they cannot afford to pay a decent daily rate.

Figure 206 shows results from my tour crew survey of a couple of years ago. The majority of touring crew earn $US 151-200, £151-200, or $AUS 101-150 a day. Now, you could use that as a yard stick when setting your price, and it's about the same as plucking a figure out of the air; what will you say if someone asks you to justify what you are asking for? You need some formula that you can use to explain how you arrived at the daily rate if you are challenged by a prospective employer about your proposed fees.

A good starting point for a formula is to take the minimum wage for your state or country, multiply it by 10 (for the average 10 hours a day you work), and then add an extra amount that you feel is appropriate, depending on your skills and experience. Suppose you live in California and you have been hired by a band that you have previously worked with, but who have just been signed to a record company. They used to pay you $50 a day with no per diems and no wage for days off. You want to take things to a more professional level with them, so you ask for $140 a day and a $15 per diem for days off. They balk at your request until you explain your reasoning: Minimum wage in the state of California is $11.00 an hour at the time of this writing. You work an average of 10 hours a day, so $11.00 x 10 = $110. Add another $30 for the skills and experience you can bring to them, and this gets you $140 per day. You then explain that you do not really need a per diem on show days because there will be food and drink provided by the promoters. However, you would like $15 per diem on the days off because there will be no supplied catering and you will have to fend for yourself. The band can either accept your offer or not; the point is that they can see the reasoning and that you are not simply doubling your fees because they now have a record company backing them.

To get to being paid $300 a day requires you explain (after some years of experience, or a couple of major tours under your belt), that minimum where is $11 where you live, and you are worth twice, or three times that amount ($11 x 3= $33), and that you still work an average of 10 hours a day ($33 x 10 - $330). In fact, a common statistic for rock n roll working hours is 18 hours a day, and I'd rather work less hours than get paid for 18 hours of work every day! [24]

I use the minimum 'wage x hours + experience' formula to set a price for everything I do - I'm not plucking a figure out the air, I have a logical reason for the amount I 'm asking for, and the amount can be negotiated within a certain range - I'm not going to work for less than minimum wage, for instance.

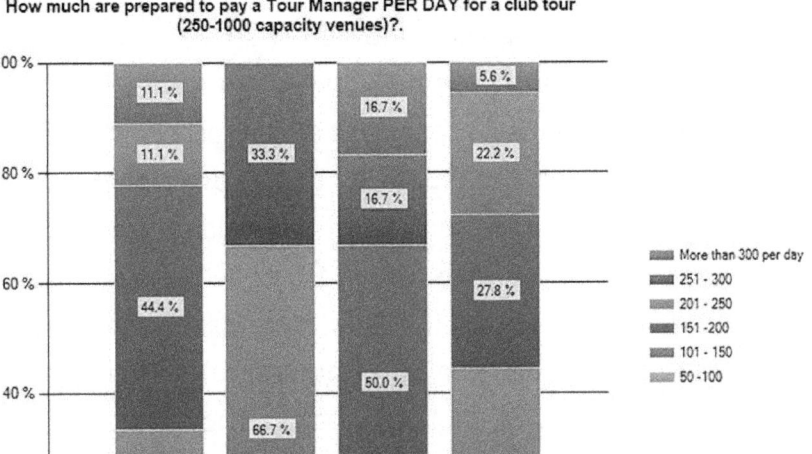

Figure 206: Survey results from asking how much road crew are paid.

Book Keeping

I am going to digress a little here as this section won't help you find or keep road crew work, and it will help you grow your business. Starting a new freelance crew business can be a hectic time, one in which it is easy to overlook the small, but important, details such as keeping your receipts and paying your invoices. Neglecting these will cause you many, many problems further down the line. Indeed, you may appear to be making lots of money but is your business in good financial health? You need to keep on top of this stuff, and this is where a book keeper comes in.

A Real Book Keeper

A book keeper is not the same thing as an accountant. Many

small business owners do employ an accountant to take care of their year-end tax returns, and quite rightly so. However, what usually happens is that the business owner just turns over a shoe-box full of receipts to their accountant at the year-end and the accountant will then charge the owner a huge amount of money to sort through the disorganised pile of bills and receipts, in order to create the year-end accounts. Aside from the massive cost, this system (or lack of) also gives the small business owner no idea of the day-to-day financial health (or otherwise) of their business. That is why you should hire a book-keeper. They are less expensive than an accountant and can help you keep in touch with your finances on a week-by-week, or month-by month, basis. She can come in for a few hours a week (or after each period of touring) to check over your receipts, enter the figures into a record keeping system and, most importantly, chase outstanding invoices for you. This will save you time and money.

You can find a good book-keeper by looking in your local business listings or, better still, asking other small businesses and freelancers who they use. You should only need to see your book keeper for a couple of hours a week at the most. It is true that having a well-ordered book-keeping system will not get you loads of road crew work; not having one will probably lead you to financial ruin.

A Software Book Keeper

An alternative to hiring a book-keeper is to use dedicated book keeping and accounting software or online service. There are numerous stand-alone or on-line offerings to choose from and, if you are disciplined enough to enter all your expenses and invoices as you go along, could be as effective as a book keeper in helping you make sure your business is making (and keeping) money. You are going to have to do some research as to which one is most suitable for you and remember - you are looking at something that will do the basic book keeping functions - receipt and expense tracking with basic invoicing - for you. Some systems integrate directly with the government tax collection departments - Freeagent in the UK (figure 306) will send your end-of year income statement and tax due calculation directly to Her Majesty's Revenue & Customs (HMRC) from within the software, saving hours of form filling. You do not need a fully featured accounting package though - just the ability to keep on top of your cash flow.

Figure 306: A software book keeping package will help you make sure your business is making (and keeping) money, if you enter all your transactions regularly.

Strategies for Getting More Work

If you follow the instructions in step 4 you will get your initial road crew work. The following strategies will help you to continue working on-the-road.

Avoid 'Cookie Cutter' Emails

This is a cardinal sin and will get you a bad reputation in a small industry. A 'cookie cutter' email is one where you cut and paste some pre-written text into numerous emails, simply changing the 'to' field, and customising the greeting (in fact, I often receive template-based emails with 'Hello', or 'Hi' as the greeting - eeesh!). If you are going to contact an artist manager (for instance) 'cold' (i.e. you have no previous dealings with them) at least undertake some basic research and find out who they manage and what artists they have on tour. The advent of email means it is easy for anyone to send off 20 or so emails and then sit back, waiting for the recipients to take action. Don't do it. Do your research, and craft each email from scratch, or only paste in a few lines about yourself. While not actually spam, cookie-cutter, work-seeking email is just as annoying as receiving a 'buy cheap Viagra' email for any music industry professional, so don't do it.

At the same time, making a cold phone call is an uncomfortable and nerve-racking process for many of us. Calling someone shows more commitment, and a desire to make a situation happen. The fact that you made a phone call instead of sending an impersonal email is always more impressive.

Make Friends With Other Crew Members and Keep in Regular Contact.

You will make friends with the crew colleagues when all working for the same artist. But what about people you meet who are working for the headliners, or other support acts? Well, the same goes. You will all get on during the day and, if time permits and it does not appear to creepy, you should initiate some swapping of phone numbers or social networking details. As well as being human nature, this interaction increases your network and will be useful in getting more work. This works because all successful tour crew get offered employment that clashes with existing work commitments. When that happens, they will have to decline the work and will be asked if they know of someone else who may be suitable and available. That person could be you. So, keep in touch with your crew buddies. Social networks have made this super-easy - there are numerous Facebook groups dedicated to touring crew, for instance (figure 406).

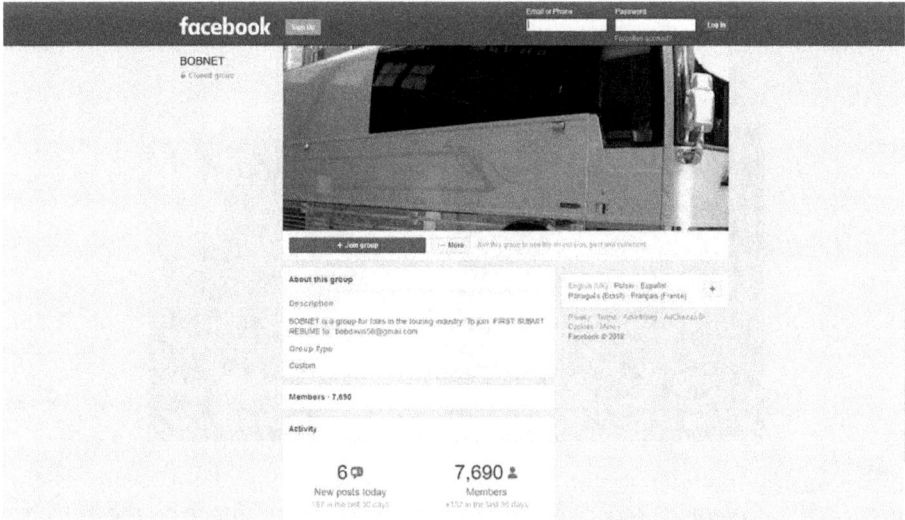

Figure 406: A typical Facebook group for touring crew.

Keep Up With Your Research

You used Hunter, LinkedIn, and perhaps a trade directory to get your first work, and now you are touring full time you should not neglect this research. Find out who is touring, when and where. Look on promoter and venue websites. Subscribe, or have access to, industry trade magazines such as Audience and Billboard, and to websites such as CelebrityAccess.com (figure 506) - these all have limited, but useful, resources included in the non-paid versions. Remember that most tours are booked between four and eight months in advance, with tickets going on sale only 2-3 months before a tour goes out. The hiring of touring crew can be done at the very last minute (as discussed elsewhere) and it does no harm to know well in advance that a tour is happening and make yourself known to the relevant artist manager or tour manager.

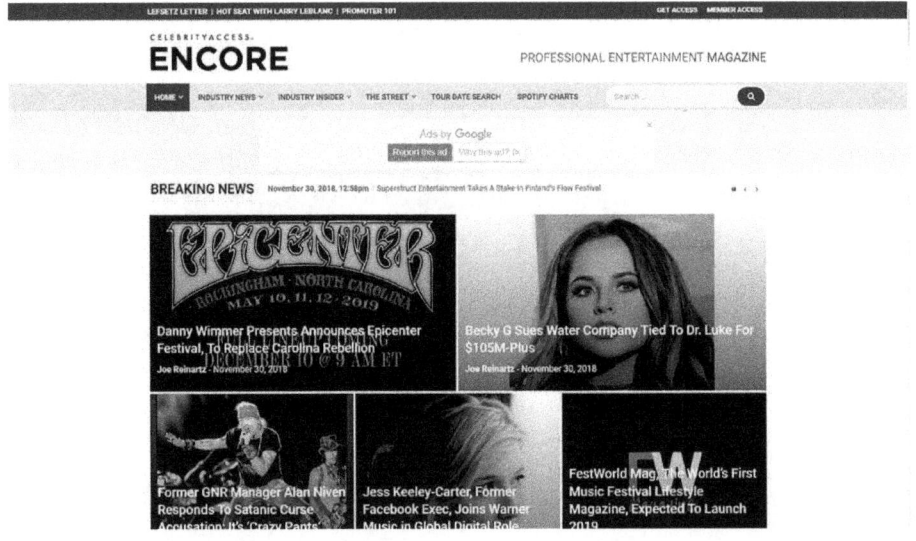

Figure 506. Celebrity Access is a great way to keep your finger on the touring pulse.

Keep in Touch with Previous Clients.

It sounds obvious but artist managers and booking agents do not really have your employment welfare at the top of their list of priorities. They will not be thinking constantly about giving you work, so to make them do so you need to keep in touch with them. Ensure you are on their 'radar' and at least appear to be genuinely interested in the career of the artist you they represent. A reminder email or call every 2-3 months should do the trick.

Get Those Recommendations

You've done a good job on tour, taken care of your cash flow and have a well-prepared functional résumé, informative web site, good social media interaction and brochures all set up to give or show to other prospective clients. Is there something you can do to really sell the idea that an artist manager should use you, as opposed to your colleague? What does an artist manager look for when selecting the people she is going to hire? According to my research, 92 % of music industry professionals hire their crew through recommendation from a trusted colleague. It's simple: To get the work you need to be recommended.

Sending unsolicited résumés, bulk email mailings, and using web-based 'crew sites' are useful to you, and top business people in the modern live music industry work from direct contact or recommendation, finding 'suppliers' (touring crew, for instance) in the same way you would an electrician or plumber - from recommendations. For example, I for one do not go around all day thinking about a list of potential plumbers I can call upon if I need to. Rather, I will find myself suddenly needing a plumber and so either: 1) look online, or better still, 2) call someone I know who has used a plumber recently and ask for a recommendation. Artist managers think in the same way about the tour crew they need. Mrs. Manager may say to herself: 'Well that's the tour planned; the band leave in eight weeks. Oh, better get a Tour Manager and a Front-Of-House engineer I suppose.' At that stage she will ask around her network and the crew people who come most highly recommended will probably get the job. You can ensure you are highly recommended by having 'testimonials' from satisfied clients included in your 'brochures' - websites, social media sites and email signatures.

Testimonials from Satisfied Clients.

Publicise your achievements by asking satisfied clients for a positive paragraph that you can put on your website and in your other brochures. These statements are called 'testimonials', and just like a good review on Amazon, they give you what's called 'social proof' (figure 606).Not only are you telling the prospective client how good you are, but other people are also saying how good you are! Testimonials are extra-ordinarily powerful, and you should go out of your way to make sure you get a testimonial for all the work you do. As soon as you have finished a tour or event, write to the person who directly employed you and ask them to jot something down for you to use in your resume or on your website. Be polite and, if necessary, write out a rough version of what you would like them to say about you. Always make sure you seek their permission to publicise any comment they may have written without solicitation, if they send you a 'thank you' email for instance. Gather your testimonials and paste them into a section on your website called 'testimonials', or 'satisfied clients'. Keep this section updated, and it will pay dividends in getting future work.

It is worth bearing in mind that we all are increasingly time-short and information hungry. A prospective client needs to know you are capable and that you have experience. You are far more likely to get work if your prospective client can check you out by simply going to a web page and getting all the information about you that she needs.

Figure 606: Testimonials give you 'social proof' - prospective clients can read comments from your satisfied customers, which shows you are great at what you do.

Conclusion

If you have followed the steps you should be in a good position to follow your dream and continue your career in the live music industry. I want to leave you with a final check list of actions, inspiration and motivational thoughts in order to fill you with energy and excitement for the road ahead (pun intended.)[25]

- Have a solid résumé. You are starting a business and may never need it, and refining and improving your resume helps you to define your skills.

- Prepare yourself mentally and spiritually to face rejection. Entering a new career and establishing a new business is not going to be easy, especially in tough economic times.

- Use your network. When things get tough you can turn to your network for help, guidance or reassurance.

- Set short-, medium- and long-term goals and keep measuring your progress towards those goals. Your freelance tour crew business may not be successful for a while and you can take comfort in the satisfaction of reaching steps along the way.

- Ask intelligent questions. You need to appear as an asset to potential clients, your touring colleagues and other music industry professionals. Asking questions not only makes you seem interested, it furthers your knowledge.

- Do your research and learn as much as you can about the way the live music industry works. Study the top promoters and booking agents to understand the 'supply and demand' of this business.

Finally, remember that thousands of people before you have followed their dream and now work as freelance crew on-the-road. You are no different from those people – if they did it, then so can you. Keep a positive attitude and you will succeed!

Appendices

Appendix 1

The following pages contain a brief list of the roles of the various people involved in creating a modern show or tour. There is no specific crew roster that a tour must have; in many cases one person will take have more than role on a tour. However, one attribute common to all these jobs is a passion for live music!

Artist management

The artist manager is responsible for overseeing every aspect of the artist's career. This is not a recognised touring position as such, but the manager will probably accompany the artist as they start out performing live. The manager will then appoint a tour manager to oversee the concert performances as the artist becomes established, then visiting the tour as it plays in key markets and more important cities.

Level of tour:
Bars to stadiums.

Qualifications or training available:
Yes. Artist management, music management and live event management degrees and training courses available.

Employment status:
Usually self-employed. Successful artist managers will then employ full-time junior managers and assistants.

Skills and personality:
- Total understanding of every aspect of the music business - record company deals, publishing deals, synchronisation deals, copyright law, radio & TV promotion, touring, offline and online marketing and branding opportunities.
- Office productivity software skills – Word, Excel, email client.
- Self-motivated.
- Established industry network.
- Good business acumen.
- Calm under pressure.
- Passionate about their artist.

Equipment needed:

Telephone, smart phone (capable of receiving emails on the move), laptop or desktop computer and a reliable internet connection.

Comments:

The manager's income is dependent on the earning potential of her artist: good artist managers will therefore set clear boundaries when it comes to responsibilities – spending all day sorting out her client's laundry or ordering taxis is not an effective, or income generating, use of the mangers time.

Booking Agent

Finds paid performance work for the artist. Not a touring position as such.

Level of tour:
Bar to stadium.

Qualifications or training available:
Not specifically. Live events management and music management course may touch on some aspects of becoming an agent. Most agents learn from mentors or from on-the-job training.

Employment status:
Self-employed initially or may join an established company as a junior booking agent.

Skills and personality:
- Total understanding of the live music business – concert promotion, contracts and riders, foreign artist taxation, visas and work permits, ticketing and merchandising. Some knowledge of tour production will also be very useful.
- Office productivity software skills – Word, Excel, email client.
- Must be able to establish and grow a network.

Equipment needed:
Telephone, smart phone (capable of receiving emails on the move), laptop or desktop computer, printer and an internet connection.

Comments:
Booking agents may have to attend gigs 4 or 5 nights a week in order to check out new talent and see existing clients.

Concert Promoter

Finds and hires venues, creates advertising and sells tickets for shows and tours. Not a touring position.

Level of tour:
Bar to stadium.

Qualifications or training available:
Yes. Live event management and show promotion courses and degrees available.

Employment status:
Self-employed initially. May join established promoter as junior promoter or assistant.

Skills and personality:
- Total understanding of the live music business – concert promotion, contracts and riders, foreign artist taxation, visas and work permits, ticketing and merchandising. Some knowledge of tour production will also be very useful.
- Office productivity software skills – Word, Excel, email client.
- Talent spotting skills.
- Good financial acumen.

Equipment needed:
Telephone, laptop or desktop computer and an internet connection.

Comments:
Promoting is a financially risky occupation. Competing events, the weather and transport problems can all affect the amount of people who turn up at a show. A successful promoter must promote as many events as possible and be ruthless in cutting costs – which sometimes is to the detriment of the artist and audience.

Promoter's Rep

Represents the promoter at each show. A rep will probably travel with the band and crew if a string of dates is being promoted by one particular promoter. In any case, promoter's reps must travel to each show they are working on.

Level of tour:
300 capacities and upwards.

Qualifications or training available:
None that is specific to this role. Live music management or events management courses may be useful.

Employment status:
Freelance.

Skills and personality:

- Total understanding of the live music business – concert promotion, contracts and riders and foreign artist taxation.
- Self-motivated.
- Responsible.
- Excellent financial skills – show settlements, taxation etc.
- Show production knowledge is very useful.
- Office productivity software skills – Word, Excel, email client.

Equipment needed:
Telephone, laptop. a device capable of sending and receiving emails on the move, portable printer, car.

Comments:
A promoter's rep has a great deal of responsibility as they not only have to make sure the show runs smoothly, they also have to take

of the payment to the artist and make sure that the promoter receives every penny left from ticket sales. Working as a rep is great way to see all sides of modern touring – reps often move into tour management.

Tour Manager

The tour manager does not book the shows but is responsible for all aspects of the planning and logistics of the tour. Travels with the band and oversees the day-to-day running of the shows.

Level of tour:
300 capacities and upwards.

Qualifications or training available:
There are no specific concert tour management courses (yet) but degrees and training are available in live event management and music management.

Employment status:
Freelance. The tour manager is usually hired by the artists themselves.

Skills and personality:
- Total understanding of the music business – concert promotion, contracts and riders, foreign artist taxation, visas and work permits, ticketing, merchandising, radio & TV promotion.
- Office productivity software skills – Word, Excel, email client.
- Financial responsibility and training.
- Self motivated
- Excellent people skills.
- Calm under pressure

Equipment needed:
Cell phone, laptop with office productivity software, a device capable of sending and receiving emails on the move, a portable printer, flash light and a bottle opener.

Comments:

Even though the tour manager is expected to have an encyclopedic knowledge of concert touring it is probably more important that they know which specialist to ask in case of an issue or challenge. The tour manager will act as tour accountant on smaller level tours (200 – 5000 capacity venues) – dealing with the payments and show settlements; this role may be taken over by a dedicated tour accountant on larger tours (see below).

Production Manager

The Production Manager is responsible for the production elements of large-scale touring: sound, light and video equipment, staging, power and associated transport.

Level of tour:
Any tour carrying its own production, usually of venues with capacities of 1500+

Qualifications or training available:
Yes.

Employment status:
Freelance. Hired directly by the artist via the tour manager.

Skills and personality:
- Complete understanding of the technical requirements of staging a modern music event.
- Employment and 'working-time' regulations
- Health and safety regulations
- Office productivity software – Word, excel, email clients
- Technical design/CAD software
- Good leader
- Stamina

Equipment needed:
Cell phone, laptop with office productivity software, a device capable of sending and receiving emails on the move, a portable printer, flash light, Personal Protective Equipment (hi-vis vest, steel cap boots, hard hat).

Comments:

No-one should underestimate the responsibility of the production manager. There have been a few high-profile accidents involving stage and rigging collapses recently, the responsibility for which lies directly with the production management. Don't put yourself forward for this role if you don't know what you are doing!

Audio Crew – Systems Tech

The system techs set-up and de-rig the sound equipment on a tour carrying its own sound equipment. The system tech is there to help and support the artist's own audio engineers. There will usually be three systems tech - a FOH 'babysitter', a monitor 'babysitter', and a 'third man'.

Level of tour:
Production level, usually venues with capacities of 2000 plus.

Qualifications or training available:
Yes. Audio and live audio training and degrees as well as manufacture specific training i.e. L-Acoustics 'Certified V-Dosc Engineer' accreditation, or Avid VENUE certification.

Employment status:
Freelance. Hired by the sound rental company. Manufacturers may also send their research and development (R&D) employees out on the road if supplying new products and technology to a rental company.

Skills and personality:
- Ability to set-up and run pro-audio equipment.
- Work as part of team.

Equipment needed:
Personal Protective Equipment (hi-vis vest, steel cap boots, hard hat), flash light, electrical multi-meter, tool kit.

Comments:
There are many specialisms now in concert audio, such as digital audio networking, and wireless ('RF') audio; anyone who has training and experience in these areas is going to stand a better

chance of working permanently. Unfortunately, system techs very rarely get to mix audio at concerts.

Audio Crew – Artist

The artist's audio engineers are hired directly by the artist to mix the Front-of-House and monitor (stage) sound for the band.

Level of tour:
Bar to stadium.

Qualifications or training available:
Yes. Audio and live audio training and degrees.

Employment status:
Freelance. Hired directly by the band.

Skills and personality:
- Ability to set-up and run pro-audio equipment.
- Mix audio to a consistently high standard.
- Work as part of team

Equipment needed:
Personal Protective Equipment (hi-vis vest, steel cap boots, hard hat), flash light, headphones, electrical multi-meter, tool kit.

Comments:
Most bands will hire a 'sound man' (audio engineer) before they consider any other crew. Working with a band from day one may not earn you much money but will give you a chance to grow with an act and (hopefully) share in the success later down the road. I recommend you go on as many manufacturer-led audio training courses as possible; those guys want to use their gear and you get to play with lots of shiny new toys!

Lighting Crew – Systems Tech

Lighting system techs operate in the same way as their audio system tech colleagues; they set-up and de-rig the lighting equipment on a tour carrying its own equipment. The system tech is there to help and support the Lighting Designer and/or operator.

Level of tour:
Production level, usually venues with capacities of 2000 plus.

Qualifications or training available:
Yes. Lighting design and technology training and degrees as well as manufacturer specific courses.

Employment status:
Freelance, hired by the lighting rental company. Manufacturers may also send their research and development (R&D) employees out on the road if supplying new products and technology to a rental company.

Skills and personality:
- Ability to set-up and run pro-lighting equipment.
- Work at heights.
- Work as part of team
- Proficiency in lighting design software, (WYSIWYG etc) is an advantage.

Equipment needed:
Personal Protective Equipment (fall-arrest harness, hi-vis vest, steel cap boots, hard hat), flash light, electrical multi-meter, tool kit.

Comments:

Lighting technology is advancing at an alarming rate as the world looks to LED and other non-tungsten technology to offset carbon emissions. Make sure you subscribe to all the relevant trade magazines and get on as many manufacturer-led training courses as possible in order to keep your knowledge current.

Lighting Crew – Lighting Director/Operator

The lighting director ('LD') creates the look and feel for the stage lighting, indicating which lamps and fixtures should go where on the stage. In the case of a small club show this design takes place in the afternoon of the show and at production level will programmed in a pre-production rehearsal some weeks in advance. The LD may then operate the show on tour or designate an operator to 'run' the various scene changes.

Level of tour:
Bar to stadium.

Qualifications or training available:
Yes. Lighting for music events courses and manufacturer-lead training available.

Employment status:
Freelance, hired directly by the band.

Skills and personality:
- Ability to design and operate a professional lighting show.
- Be confident and competent with emerging lighting control technologies.
- Work as part of a team.
- Work at heights.

Equipment needed:
Personal Protective Equipment (fall-arrest harness, hi-vis vest, steel cap boots, hard hat), flash light, electrical multi-meter, tool kit. Lighting design software and a powerful computer would be an advantage.

Comments:

Increasing integration of traditional lighting and new video technology means the modern LD needs to really keep herself up-to-date with emerging technology. Subscription to relevant trade magazines and attendance at trade shows such as PLASA (www.plasashow.com) and LDI (www.ldishow.com) is a must.

Video Crew

The video crew set-up, operate and de-rig the video elements of a modern concert. This includes video screens to enhance visibility for the audience of the artist on-stage (IMage MAGnification, or 'IMAG'), as well as video-as-lighting effects. The video crew includes screen technicians, projection technicians, vision mix operators; graphics mix operators, and camera people.

Level of tour:
Production level, usually venues with capacities of 2000 plus.

Qualifications or training available:
Yes. Video and lighting for music events courses and manufacturer-lead training available.

Employment status:
Freelance, hired by the video equipment rental company. Manufacturers may also send their research and development (R&D) employees out on the road if supplying new products and technology to a rental company.

Skills and personality:
- Ability to set-up and run pro-video projection, graphics and camera equipment.
- Work at heights.
- Work as part of team
- Proficiency in media server software an advantage.

Equipment needed:
Personal Protective Equipment (fall-arrest harness, hi-vis vest, steel cap boots, hard hat), flash light, electrical multi-meter, tool kit.

Comments:

Video is ubiquitous in modern concert touring. Lighting designers and operators are best placed to make the transition to this medium as they (should) understand colour theory and the craft of stage lighting. There is a bewildering range of technologies and disciplines in this one area, however. You must understand screen technology, LED devices, front and rear projection, media servers, and vision mixers, as well as camera operation. Training is essential.

Backline Crew

The backline crew oversee the set-up, maintenance and pack down of the artist's instruments – drums, bass, guitars, keyboards, stage computers etc, as well as the supervision of the artists stage environment – setting towels, water and set lists on stage prior to the show.

Level of tour:
Bar to stadium.

Qualifications or training available:
No specific 'backline technician' courses but you could study electrical engineering for musical and consumer devices. You should also be qualified or have extensive experience of relevant software programs (Pro Tools for instance).

Employment status:
Freelance. You will be hired by the band.

Skills and personality:
- Understanding of how a gig 'works'.
- Encyclopedic knowledge of musical instruments.
- Electrical safety.
- Knowledge of wireless ('RF') transmission for instruments.
- Work as part of team.
- Excellent people skills.
- Calm under pressure.
- Ability to fault-find and solve problems.

Equipment needed:
Personal Protective Equipment (hi-vis vest, steel cap boots, hard

hat), flash light, electrical multi-meter, tool kit and a workbox with relevant test gear for your specialism.

Comments:

You will have a close working relationship with the bands you work for as a backline tech. You, as opposed to any other crew member, will be seen by the audience on the same stage as their idols. Don't let that go your head though; you are not part of the band and you are there to do YOUR job.

Rigger

The job of the rigger is to help the sound, lighting and video system crews to 'fly' their equipment above the stage. The rigger will go into the roof of the venue to create 'points' from which steel cables and lifting motors can be attached; these are used to lift the lighting and video trusses into the air.

Level of tour:

Any tour carrying its own production, usually of venues with capacities of 2000 plus.

Qualifications or training available:

Yes. There is increasing regulation in this area – any serious rigger should make sure they are qualified or union-assessed as to their competence.

Employment status:

Freelance.

Skills and personality:

- Head for heights!
- Awareness of health and safety regulations.
- Understanding of safe working weight load limits for venue structures, motors, cables, shackles and harnesses.

Equipment needed:

Personal Protective Equipment (Fall-arrest harness, hi-vis vest, steel cap boots, hard hat).

Comments:

Riggers have an enormous responsibility these days. More rigging points and increased load-bearing components are required for shows with more staging, more video and more lighting elements.

These productions still have to load in and be set up in the same time however; this puts increasing pressure on riggers to get the points put in and the equipment flown safely.

Caterer

Touring caterers prepare hot, tasty food for appreciative road crew and unappreciative artists every day of the tour.

Level of tour:

Any tour carrying its own production (not USA), plus festivals.

Qualifications or training available:

Yes but not specifically for on-tour catering. You should have first-hand experience of working in a very busy kitchen with very demanding customers.

Employment status:

Freelance, hired by the tour catering company. May be employed full-time in the USA by a company supplying catering services to a venue.

Skills and personality:

- Good cook
- Excellent people skills
- Ability to improvise
- Stamina

Equipment needed:

Tour caterers travel with ovens, refrigerators, pots and pans, flatware and cutlery provided by the on-tour catering company. You would want your own aprons, hat and specialised knives though.

Comments:

There are not many opportunities for touring as a chef in the US as many venues have existing contracts with companies that provide food and beverage to the public as well as to the visiting artist and crew. This is not the case in Europe or Australia; however, tour caterers have being the distinction of being 'first in, last out' at any show – it is NOT a glamorous life.

Stagehand

Stagehands assist with the load-in, set up and load-out of a modern concert. Not a touring position.

Level of tour:
Bar to stadium.

Qualifications or training available:
There are some stage management and production courses. Any technical (lighting, sound etc) course will also be useful. Look at ways to expand your specialism; fork lift, Manitou operation, and rigging training, for instance.

Employment status:
Freelance.

Skills and personality:

- Work as part of team.
- Follow directions.
- Good time keeping.
- Willingness to learn.
- Work at heights.
- Stamina.
- Physical strength.

Equipment needed:
Personal Protective Equipment (hi-vis vest, steel cap boots, hard hat), adjustable spanner and a flash light.

Comments:
Being a stagehand is about as unglamorous as it gets. You will be working 12-16 hour days with little thanks. It is also the best way

to observe how a modern concert 'works' and to meet existing touring crew first hand.

Driver

Driving of vans, trucks or tour buses.

Level of tour:

Vans – bar to stadium. Trucks and buses are usually found on tours carrying their own production elements i.e. in venues with a capacity of 2000 or more.

Employment status:

Freelance. You will be hired by the trucking or busing company supplying the tour.

Skills and personality:

- Valid driving licence, no endorsements or penalty points.
- Appropriate licence for driving private, public or freight transport.
- Excellent people skills.
- Ability to work as part of team.
- Understand tour merchandise operations (see 'Comments' below)
- Ability to operate a spotlight (see 'Comments' below)

Equipment needed:

The tour transportation will usually supply the bus or truck. Some owner/operators will have their own bus or truck.

Comments:

Bus and truck drivers can make extra money on tour by helping to sell merchandise, or by operating spotlights as part of the lighting crew during the show.

Tour Security

Tour security personnel are on tour to provide security and close protection services to the touring artist, as well as advice for the safety of the entire touring party.

Level of tour:

Whenever the artist or artist's management deem it to be necessary or perceive a threat.

Qualifications or training available:

Yes. Courses in crowd management, event security and close protection are available. Many countries now require security operatives, at whatever level, to be licensed. You should enquire as to the relevant licensing where you live.

Employment status:

Freelance or maybe self-employed running your own security company.

Skills and personality:

- Relevant close protection, crowd management and crowd safety training.
- Excellent people skills.
- Self motivation.
- Stamina.

Merchandiser

A tour merchandiser sells t-shirts, CDs, buttons, posters and other tour memorabilia, on behalf of the artist at concerts.

Level of tour:
Bar to mid-level production (venues of 5000 capacity).

Qualifications or training available:
None.

Employment status:
Freelance.

Skills and personality:
- Excellent people skills.
- Excellent financial skills.
- Office productivity software skills – Word, Excel, email client.
- Good organisational skills.
- Willingness to learn.
- Aesthetic sense – able to create an inviting display of merchandise.
- Financially responsible.

Equipment needed:
Personal Protective Equipment (hi-vis vest, steel cap boots, hard hat), flash light, cash box, Sharpies, laptop computer to capture email addresses.

Comments:
The individual tour merchandiser becomes irrelevant at venues above capacities of 5000 or more. At that level the job of selling the bands merchandise is usually grabbed by the venue itself (for a percentage of the gross takings) or contracted out to a merchandis-

ing company. However, selling merch for a small to intermediate level band is still the best way to get to know the live music business and establish a network of touring contacts – just make sure you make yourself useful to the rest of the touring crew before the doors open.

Tour Accountant

A specialised touring role reserved for larger tours, the tour accountant works with the Tour Manager to oversee the collection and payment of all tour-related money.

Level of tour:
Larger production tours of venues with capacities of 10,000 plus.

Qualifications or training available:
There are no specific tour-related accountancy courses and you would have to have passed a relevant accountancy degree to be taken seriously.

Employment status:
Freelance or full-time as part of the artist's management company.

Skills and personality:
- Total understanding of the live music business —contracts and riders, foreign artist taxation, visas and work permits, ticketing and merchandising. Some knowledge of tour production will also be very useful.
- A financial accountancy degree or award.

Equipment needed:
Cell phone, laptop with office productivity software and a portable printer.

Wardrobe Assistant

Wardrobe assistants (there are no wardrobe bosses!) oversee the preparation and upkeep of stage clothes and costumes for the artist and other touring musicians, dancers and performers.

Level of tour:

Larger production tours of venues with capacities of 5,000 plus.

Qualifications or training available:

Yes but none specific to concert touring. Theatre costume design degrees will give you the necessary knowledge of stage clothing, quick changing etc.

Employment status:

Freelance.

Skills and personality:

Costume design and upkeep in a theatre/concert environment.

Excellent people skills

> Ability to work as part of team
>
> Work under pressure

Equipment needed:

Equipment for haberdashery and millinery repairs, cell phone, laptop with office productivity software and a portable printer.

Stylist

Stylists attend to the hair care and makeup for the stage performers.

Level of tour:

Larger production tours of venues with capacities of 5,000 plus.

Qualifications or training available:

Yes but none specific to concert touring. Training in beauty therapy, theatrical makeup, and hair styling will be useful.

Employment status:

Freelance.

Skills and personality:

- Hair styling, beauty make-up, and theatrical make-up in a concert backstage setting.
- Excellent people skills
- Ability to work as part of team
- Work under pressure
- Not being 'fazed' by working with very famous pop stars.

Equipment needed:

Equipment for hair and makeup styling.

Appendix 2

The following is a contract designed to set out the terms and conditions for freelance road crew work. Refer to Step 5, and the section names 'Agree the Terms of Service' to see how you would use such a contract with a client.

Freelance Crew Contract

THIS AGREEMENT is made the < *Date.* > *day of* < *Month...............* >
BETWEEN < *Insert your name or Co name* >*of* :

< *Insert your address...............................* > *(The Supplier) AND*
<*Insert your customers name* >*of* :

< *Insert your customers address................................* > *(The Client).*

CONTRACT DETAILS

CONTRACT NO: < *Insert your job No* >

EVENT, PRODUCTION OR TOUR: <*Insert name of job/tour* >

DURATION OF THE AGREEMENT:

From: <*Insert Start Date*>   To: <*Insert Finish Date*>

1. The Supplier agrees to supply goods/services in accordance with the Schedule attached hereto or as subsequently agreed in writing by the parties hereto.

2. It is hereby agreed that prior to the signing hereof The Client has had ample opportunity to examine The Supplier's Terms of Business attached hereto and shall be deemed to have unequivocally accepted them.

3. The total contract price shall be *<Insert price and currency>* plus VAT *(if applicable)*

4. The terms of payment are: *<Insert Payment terms>*

5. In the event of cancellation of this Agreement by The Client and without prejudice to any rights hereunder or under the Terms of Business attached hereto, The Client will indemnify The Supplier as a result of such cancellation for <........ >% of the contract price. Interest at a rate of < ..... >% per month is liable to be charged on any outstanding balances.

6. It is a fundamental term of this agreement that the stipulations as to payment contained be fully adhered to by The Client (including an absolute requirement of payment to be made within the times stipulated but subject to the proviso contained in Condition 4) and if for any reason The Client shall be in breach of such stipulations The Supplier shall have the right at its absolute and sole discretion and without prejudice to its other rights hereunder forthwith and without notice to dismantle remove or otherwise bring to an end any works service goods or other things supplied by the supplier hereunder and to terminate forthwith this agreement and be under no further liability hereunder to provide any of the services or goods herein agreed.

Signed for and on behalf of:

The Supplier

Date.

Signed for and on behalf of:

The Client

Date.

IN ADDITION TO SIGNING THE AGREEMENT, THE CLIENT IS REQUESTED TO INITIAL ALL PAGES OF THIS AGREEMENT, THE TERMS OF BUSINESS AND SCHEDULES, IN THE TOP RIGHT HAND CORNER

TERMS OF BUSINESS

1. All services and goods supplied by The Supplier are subject to the terms set out herein and in the Agreement attached unless varied in writing by the parties. The signing of the Agreement shall be deemed to be acceptance of these Terms of Business.

2. All works, goods and services shall be supplied by The Supplier to a good and workman like standard in accordance with the Schedule which is annexed hereto so far as the circumstances shall reasonably allow. The Client shall ensure that the Schedule complies in all respects with their requirements, or any authority or any other person or entity involved. The Supplier reserves the right to alter or amend the Schedule at any time if in the absolute discretion of The Supplier the needs of safety so require.

3. The Client must ensure that all necessary licences, consents and authorities to stage the event/s have been obtained and shall indemnify The Supplier in respect of any liability costs or claims arising therefrom.

4. The contract price shall be paid strictly in accordance with the terms

of payment contained in the Agreement.

5. The Client shall for the duration of the agreement place in force public liability insurance to a minimum indemnity of <£.................> and shall produce evidence of such insurance at the request of The Supplier.

6. The Supplier shall for the duration of the agreement place in force public liability insurance to a minimum indemnity of <£.................>and shall produce evidence of such insurance at the request of The Client.

7. Unless listed in The Suppliers Terms and Conditions, The Client shall be responsible for supplying the items or services listed is the schedules attached hereto at no cost The Supplier.

8. The Client shall ensure that all equipment provided by The Supplier is fully protected from and insured against all risks (including but not limited to, theft and malicious acts in respect to equipment) and shall produce evidence of such insurance with The Supplier's interest noted thereon at the request of The Supplier.

9. The Supplier shall not be liable in respect of any damage caused to the site(s) or venue(s) either during the event/s or as a result of the erection and/or dismantling of equipment and services unless such damage results from the negligent act or admission of The Supplier, the servants, agents or sub-contractors, or persons for whom they are responsible.

10. The Supplier shall so far as is reasonably practicable follow the Health and Safety rules and arrangements as set out in The Clients Health and Safety Policy.

11. Unless otherwise agreed in writing by both parties to this Agreement, The Supplier acknowledges and accepts that:

>The Client will not be providing First-Aid cover for The Sup-

plier or for The Suppliers employees for the duration of this agreement. The Supplier will be responsible for making First-Aid arrangements according to the standards set by the Health and Safety (First- Aid) Regulations 1981 for The Supplier and for The Suppliers employees.

12. The Supplier shall keep secret and shall not use or disclose and shall use his/her best endeavours to prevent the use or disclosure by or to any person any of The Client's or The Client's clients confidential information which came to his/her knowledge during the engagement.

The restriction shall apply during and after The Suppliers engagement without any time limit but shall cease to apply to information or knowledge which the Supplier establishes has in it's entirety become public knowledge otherwise than through the unauthorised disclosure or other breach of the Suppliers part of that restriction.

Confidential information means all confidential information relating to the organisation, finances, business activities and private activities of the Client, The Client's client and either of their employees and agents, suppliers or advisors.

The Supplier further agrees not to use any information gleaned during the term of this Agreement to directly or indirectly solicit business from any of The Client's clients.

13. The Supplier shall not be liable for any breach of the Agreement or terms hereof where such a breach was caused by or substantially contributed to by any cause beyond the control of the Supplier including (without limitation) Act of God insurrections riot civil commotion's Government or other enforceable regulations embargoes explosions strikes labour disputes fire and exceptionally adverse weather. The Supplier's sub-contractors shall be deemed to be parties to the Agreement for the purpose of obtaining the protection of this clause and The Client shall indemnify The Supplier in respect of any claim by a third party in respect of which liability is excluded by this clause provided always that The Supplier shall use its best endeavours to prevent such a breach or mitigate the effects thereof.

14. If The Client shall make any assignment for the benefit of its creditors, commit and/or fail to inform The Supplier of any act of bankruptcy or if, being a limited company, shall suffer any receiver of its assets to be appointed or upon commencement of any winding up or upon failure to pay any sum due to The Supplier whether due under this contract or otherwise upon other breach of contract by The Client, The Supplier shall be entitled to cease work immediately and to dismantle remove or otherwise bring to an end any works service goods or other things supplied by The Supplier hereunder. Upon ceasing work dismantling removing or otherwise bringing to an end any works service goods or other things supplied by The Supplier hereunder, this contract shall be deemed to have been terminated but without affecting any pre-existing rights of the parties including The Supplier's right to receive payment of the full price of the contract without deduction.

15. Any contract to which these terms apply shall be construed in accordance with the laws of England and the parties agree to accept the jurisdiction of the courts of England.

-end-

References

1 '2018 Mid-Year Special Features; Top Tours, Ticket Sales, Business Analysis', accessed 7 November 2018, https://www.pollstar.com/article/2018-mid-year-special-features-top-tours-ticket-sales-business-analysis-135890.

2 Neil Shah, 'Roadies: Unlikely Survivors in the Music Business', Wall Street Journal, 19 March 2015, sec. Arts, http://www.wsj.com/articles/roadies-unlikely-survivors-in-the-musicbusiness-1426780184.

3 Data Integration Division US Census Bureau, 'Income', accessed 24 March 2016, http://www.census.gov/hhes/www/income/income.html.

4 Chrissy Iley, 'The Day the Music Died', The Sunday Times, 17 June 2012, https://www.thetimes.co.uk/article/the-day-the-music-died-bxjn9z6x9gx.

5 'Live Nation Sells 85m Tickets in 2018 so Far, Posts Record Quarterly Revenue of $3.8bn', Music Business Worldwide, 2

November 2018, https://www.musicbusinessworldwide.com/livenationsells-85m-tickets-in-2018-so-far-posts-record-quarterly-revenue-of-3-8bn/.

6 David Randall, 'The Top-Earning Musicians Of 2010', Forbes, accessed 7 November 2018, 2010/07/16/u2-lady-gaga-ac-dc-business-entertainment-top-earning-musicians.

7 '2017 Year End Special Features: Top Tours, Promoters, Venues, Grosses', accessed 7 November 2018,https://www.pollstar.com/News/2017-year-end-special-features-top-tours-promoters-venuesgrosses-134154.

8 'Live Nation: Music's next Big Act', The Independent, 5 February 2009,http://www.independent.co.uk/news/business/analysis-and-features/live-nation-musics-next-bigact-1546426.html.

9 'Booking Agency Directory 2018 Summer Edition', Pollstar, accessed 5 November 2018,http://www.pollstar.com/booking-agency-directory-2018-summer-edition.

10 International Entertainment Buyers Association, 'Agents Power Panel' (Nashville, TN, October 2017).

11 '2017 Year End Special Features: Top Tours, Promoters, Venues, Grosses', accessed 7 November 2018, https://www.pollstar.com/News/2017-year-end-special-features-top-tours-promoters-venuesgrosses-134154.

12 'Concerts : Live Nation Entertainment', accessed 8 November 2018,http://www.livenationentertainment.com/concerts.

13 Kevin M. Mitchell, 'Production Profile', Front Of House, accessed 9 November 2018,http://digitaleditiononline.com/article/Production+Profile/2457204/298163/article.html.

14 'Passport Fees', accessed 12 November 2018, https://travel.state.gov/content/travel/en/passports/requirements/fees.html.

15 Flanagan 'What's It Like to Be A Modern-Day Roadie?', Text, Billboard, 30 March 2016, https://www.billboard.com/biz/articles/7317959/whats-it-like-to-be-a-modern-day-roadie.

16 Adam Zendel, 'Living The Dream: Precarious Labour in the Live Music Industry' (University of Toronto, 2014),https://tspace.library.utoronto.ca/bitstream/1807/68834/1/Zendel_Adam_M_201411_MA_thesis.pdf.

17 'Tour Life: Brian Forst - Stage Manager/Guitar Tech for Less Than Jake | Stars and Scars', accessed 5December 2018, http://starsandscars.com/tour-life-brian-forst-stage-manager-guitar-tech-less-than-jake/.

18 '10 Tech Tips from Touring Pros', accessed 5 December 2018, https://www.premierguitar.com/articles/10_Tech_Tips_from_Touring_Pros.

19 Robert W. Bly, Selling Your Services (New York: Henry Holt & Company LLC, 1991).

20 MarketingResearch Chart: How Do Customers Want to Communicate?', MarketingSherpa, 3 February 2015,https://www.marketingsherpa.com/article/case-study/customer-communication-by-channel.

21 Michael Stelzner, '2015 Social Media Marketing Industry Report' (Social Media Examiner, May 2015).

22 Josh Turner, Connect: The Secret LinkedIn Playbook To Generate Leads, Build Relationships, And Dramatically Increase Your Sales (Lioncrest Publishing, 2015).

23 Robert W. Bly, Selling Your Services (New York: Henry Holt & Company LLC, 1991).

24 Neil Shah, 'A Day in the Life of a Roadie', WSJ (blog), 19 March 2015,https://blogs.wsj.com/speakeasy/2015/03/19/a-day-in-the-life-of-a-roadie/.

25 Adapted from 'How to get A Job In The Music Industry', Hatscheck,K. Berklee

About the Author

Andy Reynolds has worked as an international concert tour manager and audio engineer for over 25 years. He has toured continuously during this time, working on an average of 200 shows per year. Andy has worked for such artists including George FitzGerald, Maribou State, The Pierces, Maverick Sabre, All-American Rejects, House of Pain, Machine Head, Nightmares On Wax, Pavement, Roots Manuva, Super Furry Animals, Skunk Anansie, and Squarepusher, as well as tours with U2, Whitney Houston, Manic Street Preachers, and Foo Fighters. His touring experience encompasses stadiums, arenas, theatres, pubs, bars, clubs, outdoor festivals, rooftops, subway stations, cruise ships, mountainsides, and very, very, muddy fields.

Learn more about Andy at **www.livemusicbusiness.com**

Please Leave a Review

I hope you enjoyed this book and found it useful. I also hope you will want to leave a review on Amazon. Your support and opinion matters to me, and it makes a difference to everything I do.

So, if you'd like to leave a review then you should go to this book's Amazon page where you will see a a big button that says, 'Write a customer review'. Please click that and you will be able to tell other readers what you didn't, or did, like about this book. Thanks again for reading.

Andy

CPSIA information can be obtained
at www.ICGtesting.com
Printed in the USA
LVHW081816020120
642352LV00038B/1457/P